Mentoring Reversed:
The Road to Creativity and Imagination

Peter Gregoire

Proverse Hong Kong
2017

Reverse mentoring has been doing the rounds in the corporate world for some years now, where it is used to introduce senior management to new technology and social media as business tools. Yet this only scratches the surface of what reverse mentoring can achieve.

Throwing two generations together in a reverse mentoring relationship creates one of the most powerful problem-solving dynamics at our disposal. It also provides a means for lifelong learning and controlled imagination. Most importantly, it can act as a key step in the character development of both participants and an opportunity for both to reflect on their true purpose in life.

MENTORING REVERSED demonstrates how, through reverse mentoring, it is possible to build a deep understanding across generations and embed the values of diversity, humility, creativity and imagination into the culture of any organization.

PETER GREGOIRE is a lawyer and author who lives and works in Hong Kong. His previous books include bestselling novels *The Devil You Know* and *Article 109*. Peter is a previous winner of the Proverse Prize and the *Standard*/RTHK short-story competition. His Tedx talk 'The Road to Imagination and Creativity? About Reverse Mentoring' can be viewed on YouTubc and serves as the inspiration for this current work, which he dedicates to his cousin Anthony Fernandes.

Mentoring Reversed

The Road to Creativity and Imagination

Peter Gregoire

Proverse Hong Kong

Mentoring Reversed
The Road to Creativity and Imagination
by Peter Gregoire.
Copyright © Proverse Hong Kong November 2017.
Alternate edition published in Hong Kong by Proverse Hong Kong.
ISBN 978-988-8228-24-9
Available through: https://www.createspace.com/6806403

First published in paperback in Hong Kong
by Proverse Hong Kong, November 2017.
Copyright © Proverse Hong Kong, November 2017.
ISBN: 978-988-8228-74-4

Distribution and other enquiries to:
Proverse Hong Kong, P.O. Box 259, Tung Chung Post Office,
Tung Chung, Lantau Island, NT, Hong Kong SAR, China.
Email: proverse@netvigator.com; Web:
www.proversepublishing.com

The right of Peter Gregoire to be identified
as the author of this work
has been asserted by him in accordance with
the Copyright, Designs and Patents Act 1988.

Cover image and design by LOL Design Ltd.

British Library Cataloguing in Publication Data
A catalogue record is available from the British Library

Contents

Part I: Opening statement

Part II: Presenting the evidence

Part III: Closing arguments

PART I

OPENING STATEMENT

Chapter 1

THE PARADOX OF EXPERIENCE

Experience is the ultimate tradable commodity in our society.

Résumé achievements dictate our value in the employment market. That's why we spend our formative years building our CVs. We start by collecting a host of academic qualifications, then graduate to piling up increasingly impressive job titles at blue-chip companies. Each new height we scale is aimed at one thing: convincing future employers of our worth.

Our key selling point is simple: "I have been tried and tested in the exact disciplines you want. I have overcome the hurdles your business needs to surmount. I've done it before for others, so I can do it again for you. I am of value to you, because of my experience".

Promotions are decided by this same formula. We move up the career ladder by convincing our bosses that we are ready because of the experience we have gained in our apprenticeship. This, we pitch, makes us the safe bet. We can be relied on to step into the shoes of the outgoing master and do the job just as well. Underpinning this is an implicit threat: if I am not chosen, there are plenty of other employers out there who will choose me.

The value we place on experience is evident in every aspect of our society. Politicians vaunt their "proven track-records" come election time. In the military, front-line soldiers who are already battle-hardened put fear into the enemy and are prized by those in command. They know what it's like to be under fire and can be trusted to fight and not be put to flight. In sports too, it is teams with experience who commentators say won't wilt under pressure at the crucial point in the season. "They have been here before and can handle being in the spotlight." Journeymen team mates are of value because they have been out on the field so many times there's no situation to which they can't react. They can settle the nerves of their younger team mates.

When a sports person without experience makes it big, we question the achievement and start picking on his or her fragilities. Iron Mike Tyson, after becoming heavy-weight champion of the world, was "too inexperienced" to see how his entourage of sycophants were taking him for a ride. This would eventually be the source of his downfall, and the source of many an "I told you so". No sooner had Leicester City won the English Premier League in 2016 than people who vaunted it as an incredible achievement were in the same breath calling it a one-off, predicting that "normal service" would be resumed the following season when the big four teams would dominate once more. Most famously of all, Alan Hansen said of Manchester United that you cannot win a championship with kids.

It's the same when we are shopping or going to the doctor or choosing any form of professional service. Recommendations from others who speak highly of their experience are the key drivers of our decision-making. We see chart-topping films precisely because of what makes them chart-topping. The fact that there are numerous others who have already experienced it, suggests it must be good. We decide what to read based on the number of good reviews a book has on amazon. The measure of experience, based on the volume of people who have actually experienced something is how trends are set. In fact, that thousands of people are experiencing it, is the very definition of a "trend".

The commodity of experience comes with associated traits which underpin its value. People with experience are able to see things through to the end. They are able to endure through hard times. They can be relied on to perform at a high level with consistency for the long-term. They can be trusted.

Further, the equation is underpinned by a cycle of virtue. A person who has spent years honing his craft, through the good times and the bad, carrying out his duty no matter what, putting in the hours of work to master what he or she is doing, deserves respect and elevation to a higher position in our social structure. This is what builds character. If only all people had the ability "to stick with it", the world would be a better place.

In short, experience equals credibility. People pay for credibility. It's that simple.

The problem with experience

But is experience really all that it's cracked up to be?

For the most part, yes, the formula of "experience = credibility" works. We need people with experience, along with all its associated traits, at the decision-making table. Without them, things simply wouldn't get done. Society would cease to function. At the same time, we need to recognize that experience has its limitations and this makes over-reliance on it counter-productive.

These limitations can be identified by interpreting exactly what it is that a person means, when he says, "I have experience." He is essentially asserting that he has the ability to execute, in the future, the same thing he has done in the past, with the same result. He is saying that he has done it before and so, the likelihood is, he can do it again. If he has done it more than once before, he has further established his reliability to replicate the experience. He can, in short, be trusted to repeat the same thing, over and over again, with limited risk of him doing anything different or achieving any different outcome.

Put in this way, we can see how reliance on experience carries with it a deep-seated conservatism, a bias in favour of keeping things as they are and not allowing, or even wanting them to change. That is the restraining element which comes in-built with experience. That is the natural boundary experience sets.

We see this conservatism in the verbiage commentators use to praise the positive aspects of experience, albeit every such positive aspect comes with a negative flipside. For example, "staying with what we know" is viewed as a positive, even though it means not trying anything new. Being a "safe pair of hands" means being reliable, but it also means being relied on not to risk trying something different. Experienced people may be called "solid", to denote their strength to get done the things we expect of them (an evident positive), but nothing more than this (sometimes, a negative). Many businesses in their appraisal system only give average bonuses to people who fall within the "solid" bracket, with the big money reserved for those who "out-perform" and achieve things beyond expectation.

Having a "proven track-record" and being "reliable" means being relied on to stay on the exact same track going forward, even where to do so is obviously wrong. The trait of "discipline" also comes with inflexibility. Having "endurance" and being able to "stick to your guns" mean an ability to endure and perpetuate the status quo.

We can see, then, that the flipside of experience is a bias against change. It is a bias against creativity, imagination and innovation, three traits which are just as important as experience, to enable society to achieve progression.

This is not to say that experience should be ignored in favour of constantly breaking from the past and taking risks to achieve great leaps forward. Doing this can have disastrous consequences. Constant innovation means total disruption and total disruption leads to complete chaos. At the same time, we need to recognise that, whilst experience may give us stability, an over-reliance on experience stifles creativity, innovation and progress.

The key is to achieve the right balance between experience on the one hand and creativity on the other, but finding that balance is particularly difficult to strike.

The paradox of experience
The difficulty arises from the generational divide which the equation "experience = credibility" prises open. Experience, by definition, is something that it takes a long time to acquire, often years of dedication and effort. The more time a person spends on a skill, the more that skill becomes hard-wired into their neural passages. This is how muscle-memory and intuition is developed, when we can perform a skill to a high standard without even thinking. However, as our brains deepen with experience, the more conditioned we become to the in-built restraints and limitations of that experience. The road to experience, in this respect, aligns perfectly with the aging process.

According to renowned brain scientist Dr Jill Bolte Taylor, the human brain does not reach its full state of maturity until a person is twenty-five years old. Until that point in time, we all possess this natural unlimited ability to imagine. The child-like mind is completely open and sees everything in the world with fresh eyes. A child is filled with wonder and awe at every new experience. He entertains every new thing he sees and is always asking questions. A child pushes boundaries, precisely because he has no idea where the boundaries lie. He sees a book shelf, he wants to climb up it, blissfully unaware of the risk of falling down. He wants to run in the street, despite the dangers of traffic. When children play, there are no limits. Paint, cotton-wool, grain, baking powder and sofa cushions, things which do not belong together, all get rolled into one giant mess, much to the consternation of parents. But this is disruptive creativity at its most elemental, taking items which an adult's mind wouldn't associate together, and mixing them with each other to see what you get. A new idea is often nothing more than the casual association of two existing but unrelated elements. Put simply, the untainted, child-like mind is naturally inventive.

As we get older, however, this changes precisely because we develop our own experience and opinions which bring with them restraints and limitations that close our minds off to new things. Slowly that natural child-like imagination becomes trapped. Where once we were the mischievous child climbing the book-shelf, now we are the harassed and fearful parent shouting "get down!" Where once, we were open to everything that was new in the world, now we are curmudgeons, disappointed at the path the youth of today is taking with all this new-fangled technology at their disposal. Instead of looking forward with optimism, we hark back to the seemingly golden age of our youth, when everything seemed so much better.

This point – the moment we stop looking forward to the future and start harking back to the past – is the defining transition to middle-age. This is the moment where we catch ourselves by saying: "Oh my God, I've become exactly like my parents!"

The problem is that when you look at the leaders and decision-makers in our society, you see a huge over-representation from people who have reached middle-age. Why? Precisely because of our over-reliance on the equation of "experience = credibility".

The result, then, gives us this paradox. We need experienced people at the helm in our society to solve some of the bigger life-and-death problems society faces. These problems, however, often need creative, inventive and imaginative solutions. Yet the leaders we call upon to be imaginative become our chosen problem-solvers when they have reached the least imaginative point in their lives precisely because of the experience which got them there.

And that's the problem. That's the paradox of experience.

Reverse mentoring

It is my contention that the paradox of experience can be solved by a dynamic called "reverse mentoring".

Reverse mentoring turns the concept of traditional mentoring on its head. In reverse mentoring a young inexperienced person mentors an older experienced person, by introducing the older person to new concepts and showing him what today's world looks like through youthful eyes.

Equipped with this refreshing outlook, the older protégé rediscovers the youthful imagination he once possessed, but is now able to combine it with years of experience to produce a practical creativity. Equally beneficial is the fact that the younger mentor obtains the opportunity to test his ideas against the reality-check embedded within his older protégé's experience, gaining priceless feedback on how to bring cutting-edge ideas to fruition.

Reverse mentoring has been doing the rounds in the corporate world for some years now, where it is used to introduce senior management to new technology and social media as business tools. In my view, although laudable, this only scratches the surface of what reverse mentoring can achieve. It is my contention that reverse mentoring can go so much further than this.

Throwing two generations together in a reverse mentoring relationship could possibly create the most powerful problem-solving dynamic at our disposal. It provides a means for lifelong learning and controlled imagination. Most importantly it can act as a key step in the character development of both participants and an opportunity for both to reflect on their true purpose in life.

In the following pages, which consist of a series of standalone essays on the subject, I set out to prove each of these assertions.

PART II

PRESENTING THE EVIDENCE

Chapter 2

THE LIMITS OF EXPERIENCE EXPOSED

September 2014 was a tumultuous month in Hong Kong's history.

Once a British colony, now a special administrative region within the People's Republic of China, Hong Kong's existence is predicated on a contradiction known as "one-country two systems". This principle couples the preservation of a British common law legal system, based on judicial independence and the rights of the individual, with the overarching governance of the largest surviving (and some say thriving) Communist state in the world.

"One-country two-systems" was paramount leader Deng Xiao Peng's formula for re-absorbing Hong Kong back into the Chinese fold in 1997, without causing undue international concern from the human rights watchers. As with any contradiction, however, one-country two-systems creates regular points of friction. The Hong Kong population, brought up on a diet of individualist economics and free speech, is finding it difficult to adapt to the Confucian mind-set of the Communist régime governing from Beijing, where individual interest is subordinate to the collective, and maintaining stability trumps all. Stuck in the middle of this contradiction is the Chief Executive of Hong Kong, appointed by Beijing to administer the Hong Kong special administrative region.

September 2014 was the month when the friction sparked into chaos. It all started with school and university students boycotting their classes in protest at the Hong Kong government's attempt to introduce a new voting system for the Hong Kong Chief Executive position. The proposed new voting system would essentially limit the candidates in the election to two or three persons pre-selected by a nominating committee which was ultimately controlled by the Chinese central government.

This was nothing more than totalitarianism with a democratic veneer, as far as the students were concerned, and they wanted to scupper it, even if it meant sticking with the status quo, where the Chief Executive was chosen by a 1,200 election committee controlled by the Central Government. Continuing with this blatant and universally ridiculed pig of totalitarianism would at least guarantee change in the future, whereas decorating the pig with a smear of democratic lipstick now might end this hope forever, was how the students thought.

The boycott reached its emotive pinnacle when the students stormed Civic Square. The consequent police reaction (it took about ten of them to arrest the student leader, a skinny individual called Joshua Wong) drew hundreds down to the protest site. Out came the pepper spray as the police tried to make the protestors back off. In response, the protestors unfurled their umbrellas and held their ground.

On the afternoon of Sunday 28 September 2014, the Hong Kong police escalated matters by doing something which they hadn't done in a long time. They fired tear-gas at the citizens who paid the taxes which financed their salaries. This was the turning point. The moment when the police crossed a line which should never have been crossed, as far as many Hong Kongers were concerned. Many law-abiding citizens, sitting at home watching events unfold, felt their anger boil over as the canisters arced their way into the crowds on their TV sets. Enough was enough, and out they went onto the streets to join the fray.

The decision to use tear-gas turned out to be a strategic mistake. Rather than clearing the crowds, it magnified them and catapulted the growing protest to the top of the global news cycle, at the very moment when China was preparing to celebrate the 65th anniversary of the founding of the

People's Republic. Branded "the Umbrella Movement", after the simple implement of daily use, which people were using to ward off pepper spray, tear gas and the rain, the student protestors had carried off a public relations coup and in the ensuing forty-eight hours, they took full advantage. The police backed off and the world looked on with a degree of admiration as the thousands of young protestors cleaned up rubbish and acted with dignity, personifying the powerful impact of peaceful civil disobedience.

The point of reciting these events here is not to establish any kind of political point, because the result of the Umbrella Movement has not seen a clean sweep for democracy in Hong Kong, far from it in fact. Beyond the politics of it all, however, what the Umbrella Movement showed us was the combustible result of placing over-reliance on the trait of "experience" in our society and ignoring its inherent limitations

The youngsters who had architected the entire protest were the product of a Hong Kong education system in which many had begun to lose faith, geared as it was towards compliance, rote learning and grade accumulation at the expense of creativity. Yet here on the streets was a generation produced by this system, acting as the epitome of creative individualist thinking. Their strategy and use of social media to organize themselves had left the police outmaneuvered. Their organization, teamwork and flexibility to adapt, as the situation played out, to win the media war, were impressive.

The "yellow umbrella" became the logo of their movement and it went viral almost overnight, achieving global awareness as Facebook users changed their profile pictures en masse to show support. Businesses routinely shell out millions of dollars for this kind of brand recognition. These students had achieved it with no budget and in a matter of hours.

They had achieved all of this, without any experience whatsoever on their side. Unrestrained by the limits of experience, they had completely outplayed a Hong Kong governmental organization which had made experience its bastion.

To get on in the Hong Kong government, experience is everything. Promotion is based on longevity of tenure and a proven track-record. Yet in the face of the youthful creativity of the Umbrella Movement, this experience counted for nothing. The experienced personnel, paid to administer Hong Kong society and preserve the rule of law, were completely bereft of a solution.

To demonstrate that they were listening, a live television debate was organized between three key government officials and the student leaders. If this had been an attempt to display the student's ignorance it completely back-fired, for the student leaders came across as articulate and polite in putting across well thought out points. By contrast, the government trio (or duo, as only two of them actually spoke) came across as out of touch and slightly patronizing.

We've heard it all before

What happened in the following months served only to underpin further the limits of experience, as the generation divide opened up into an unbridgeable chasm.

The Umbrella Movement stayed put on the streets and spread to other parts of Hong Kong, like Mong Kok where the protest was hi-jacked by thugs on both sides and dissolved in violence. At Mong Kok it was clear that an older generation of have-nots were driving the protest, rather than the students. There, the students came up against angry shop-owners and Triad gang members who looked to clear the streets in the only way they knew how. The result was mob thuggery. Again the police, under immense pressure, struggled to gain control.

Back at the main protest site, although a large phalanx of students stayed put, the media spotlight eventually moved on and support began to dwindle as citizens needed to use the highways to get back to work. Eventually, after several months, the roads reopened with the protest whimpering on until eventually petering out altogether.

Although this was not the ending it desired, the Umbrella Movement changed Hong Kong society, cleaving it cleanly down the middle into two polarized factions. From then on, you were either pro-Beijing or pro-Democracy. You were either supportive of everything the police had done or anti- the rule of law. You were either a blue umbrella (status quo) or a yellow umbrella (radical change).

In the midst of this polarization emerged a view that something had to be done about the youth of Hong Kong, that it was socio-economic conditions which had driven them onto the streets in the first place, as all they had to look forward to was a life of sitting in an office cubicle, earning a pittance of a wage, funding an increasingly ageing population and not being able to afford anywhere to live.

What followed was the typical government response to such self-diagnosed problems. Funds were thrown at commissions and committees and think-tanks given the role of "developing", "mentoring", and "nurturing" youth so as to provide them with the upward social mobility it was thought they desired. The aim was to offer the young people contentment and bring them into the fold. An Innovation and Technology Bureau was set up to help young people who were good at science find a place in the world. Exchange schemes with Mainland China and other countries were rapidly created.

Yet again, however, these supposed solutions exposed the limits of experience, for underlying the establishment's entire response lay the assumption that there was something wrong with Hong Kong youth, that what had happened was their fault. There was, the establishment thought, a defect inherent with the younger generation which could be fixed by throwing money, committees, schemes and other such vehicles at the problem. We saw this in the verbiage of every press announcement ushering in each new initiative. Young people were, we were constantly informed, "the future of Hong Kong".

This, however, completely ignored the key lesson of the Umbrella Movement, which – if nothing else – had demonstrated how innovative, creative and intelligent students in Hong Kong are today. They had out-thought, out-strategized and out-debated those with experience. Trotting out the sound bite which referred to anyone under twenty-four years old as "the future of Hong Kong" meant that the establishment was completely ignoring the fact that the youth of Hong Kong were an asset to be utilized in the present. That, instead of seeing them as the problem, we should instead be using their obvious talents to inspire a solution.

The real question which everyone should have been asking was: how can we harness the evident talents of young people, not in the future, but right now?

The baking-soda game

One of the perennial challenges of any parent in this age of technology is how to keep your kid away from an electronic device for any length of time. No easy task, I'm sure any mum or dad would agree, although curiously this has led to the resurrection of games heralding from a simpler era.

One such game involves paint, water, baking soda and a long glass. You fill the long glass with water and mix in the paint. As soon as the water is settled, you stir in the baking soda and let science take its course! A few seconds later a colourful froth surges upwards and explodes out of the glass like something from a B-grade horror movie, delighting your five-year-old no end.

I was supervising my son in carrying out this experiment one day, when I started reflecting on the Umbrella Movement which had, by that time, petered out into a straggling gang of recalcitrant unwashed campers, squatting outside the Hong Kong government offices. It seemed a pitiful ending to an event in Hong Kong's history which had originally generated such a sense of elation across many levels of society.

I had experienced that elation first-hand on those few occasions I had gone down to the protest site to witness events unfold. My first such sojourn was on 1 October 2014, the night after the police had backed off, following their misjudged use of tear gas. Thousands of people were out in the streets. The roads were completely blocked off and the whole thing had the atmosphere of a make-shift carnival. Someone was making hot-dogs on the side of the road, crates of water were being shipped hither and thither, bands were entertaining for free and spontaneous lectures on civil disobedience were conjoining. Cleanliness and politeness were top of the protest agenda that night, as it was important for the world to see how civilized those asking for change were acting. The whole thing made a powerful statement and the world's media were lapping it up.

What struck me most during that heady atmosphere, was the age of the protestors. Their youth was palpable, astonishing and embarrassing. I couldn't help but feel the failure for which my generation – the ones with the experience – were responsible. Yet at the same time, I experienced a sense of pure exhilaration. Here were my assumptions about the effects of Hong Kong's rote-learning education system being blown apart before my eyes. Before, I had thought the Hong Kong school system was almost designed to drum the creativity out of kids, by cramming their heads full of useless facts and formulas which they could regurgitate on demand at exam time. But the Umbrella Movement taught me something different.

The Hong Kong education system may indeed have aimed for the suppression of that natural child-like creativity that exists in us all up to the age of 25. But the Umbrella Movement demonstrated how the whole thing had backfired in the face of this system. All this education system had done was to put a lid on this natural resource of creativity as it simmered and boiled, to the point where it had now erupted on to our streets.

I don't know why, but that sense of exhilaration I felt, just watching those young people demonstrate their capability, lived with me for weeks and months after I left the protest site. That positivity somehow beneficially impacted my entire outlook on life. I found myself able to recapture an element of the restless energy I myself had felt when I had been the protesters' age.

Having regained that energy, I allowed it to stimulate the experience I had built up on my journey to middle age. At work, for example, I discovered a rekindled passion for what I was doing and went beyond expectations in my work product. Where before I was content just to do what had been asked of me, now I began to question things. I used my knowledge of the processes which I had previously blindly followed, to modify them for the better. Somehow, my newfound energy enabled me to channel my experience out in new and unexpected directions.

It was at this point that my mind drifted back to the experiment game my son was playing and an obvious analogy came to me. Before the protests, it was as if my life had been like that mix of water and paint, content to exist in a settled state of boredom. The exhilaration which the protest had generated within me, was like mixing in the baking soda, energizing my experience with a shot of adrenalin, sending it surging and frothing in all directions in search of something new.

That's when it hit me: the realization of how we should be tapping the natural, restless, imagination of our young people in the present, rather than just dismissing them as "the future of Hong Kong".

It had to start with my generation appreciating that our experience came with restraints and that those restraints held back our creativity. What I had feared the Hong Kong school system was doing to our kids – the bias in favour of CV experience – had actually already had this impact on my generation. By gaining experience to sell ourselves, we had become trapped by that experience and were driven to repeat that experience again and again, considering it the way to success.

Instead, what we as a generation needed to do was to find a way of unleashing that experience from its natural constraints. We, the experienced generation, needed to break free from the control which our experience had placed on us. We needed to find a method for removing the mental limits that our years of experience had imposed. We needed our experience to be unleashed in the creative search for practical solutions to the bigger problems our society faced. The experience of the older generation on its own stifled progress. But combine that experience with the natural child-like imagination and energy of youth, and you had the most powerful problem-solving dynamic at our disposal.

The only question was, how do we do it? How do we find that perfect blend of experience and youth?

As soon as I asked the question, the answer hit me like a runaway freight train.

How stupid I had been for not seeing it!

This had happened to me before in the most unexpected, fun and tragic way.

Chapter 3

THE INSPIRATION OF YOUTH

My cousin Anthony and I first met in 2003, the year I arrived in Hong Kong.

We are cousins because my mum and his dad are brother and sister, two of eleven siblings in fact, with my mother being the eldest and Anthony's dad being down at number seven. The significant age gap between them, translates into a more significant age gap between Anthony and myself. When we first met, Anthony was eight years old and I was thirty-one.

Age isn't the only difference separating us. Anthony's mum is Korean. My dad is British. We couldn't have looked or been more different, if we'd tried. Whenever we were together the fact that we were cousins took a lot of explaining, especially from me as the older one. I always felt people's skepticism boring into to me when I tried to convince them that we were related and that I wasn't trying to kidnap him!

I was still unattached when I first met Anthony. Rarely did I have to interact with children, but when I was forced to, I always did so with that awkward fear of the unknown which many singletons have when it comes to kids. Anthony sensed that fear and took full advantage of it, that was the kind of kid he was. We're not talking Norman Rockwell 'happy cutesy' families here. Anthony could be a giant pain in the butt when he wanted to be, which was most of the time.

Truth be told, discipline wasn't high on Anthony's agenda when he was eight years old. In fact his life was in a very sad place back then. Anthony's dad, my uncle David, had cancer, and had only a matter of months to live. It was a hell of a thing for any eight year old to have to come to terms with.

Uncle David passed away in 2004. I was there at hospital that day and I shall never forget the moment when Anthony said goodbye to his father for the last time. It was heartbreaking to watch and yet at the same time, one of the most courageous things I've ever been privileged to witness. All around friends and relatives were breaking down with grief, and in the midst of it all was Anthony, being stoic, resolute and not shedding a tear.

I took Anthony for a walk outside the hospital that day, to try to give him a break from it all. Anthony didn't say much to me on that walk and I knew not to disturb him because, well, I just didn't have the words. But as I watched Anthony become lost in his own thought process, I saw a change come over him. His shoulders went back, his chin was up, his jaw set. There was a defiance about him, a kind of resolution that made him stand a little taller in spite of the devastating loss he had just experienced.

Later that day, as were heading home, Anthony told me what he had been thinking in that moment. He had been making a silent promise to his father that he would become the best human being he could be, that he would grow up to make his father proud.

The telling wisdom which my eight-year old cousin displayed in that moment was astonishing. It was a wisdom which held a valuable lesson for me, that no matter how bad life gets, you roll with the punches. You don't make excuses. You carry on. Deep down, my cousin had the stuff of character and how I came to admire him for it.

The bus to nowhere
In the years that followed, I began to see more of Anthony. Anthony's mum, Christine, worked at the Korean Catholic church and Saturday was her busiest day, so often I'd meet up with Anthony and we would do things together.

Anthony was nine years old now and had developed an obsession with buses that a lot of kids that age have. He had a book which contained the history of every bus there had ever been on the Hong Kong streets and he insisted I test him on every fact it held. Wheel size, number of seats, year it went into and out of service, he had memorized the whole thing. Naturally on our first Saturday together, when I asked Anthony what he wanted to do, he said: "I want to take a bus".

"Where?" I asked

"Who cares?" he said. "Let's just take a bus."

So we did. We got on the first bus that came along and off we went.

Taking a bus, just for the sake of it, was something I had never done before, but within minutes I realized how incredibly liberating an experience it could be. We had no idea where we were going and hence no idea what to expect. Everything became tinged with excitement.

This, then, became our regular Saturday afternoon thing. We used to go to a random bus-stop and wait for the first double-decker to come along, get on, and sit on the top deck right at the front with the big windscreen. It was like having our own personal cinema showing snippets of life as we travelled across Hong Kong.

We saw all sorts of things. Market stall holders arguing with customers. Boyfriends and girlfriends walking arm in arm. Old ladies pushing carts full of cardboard through traffic. Harassed mothers elbowing their way through crowds. School kids collecting for charity. Incense burning. Queues outside the latest new restaurant. And crowds of people just going about their lives in this incredible dense intense city we called home.

To amuse ourselves, we also used to make up stories about the people we saw down on the streets. One time, Anthony pointed out the window and asked me: "What do you think that woman's carrying in her bag?"

"Looks like a watermelon." I would always start off with a boring answer.

"I think it's her husband's head," he said, upping the ante. "I think she's cut it off and she's going to throw it away."

In the spirit of "If you can't beat 'em, join 'em", I started to play along.

"No, she's not going to throw it away," I said. "I think she's going bowling with it".

"Bowling with her husband's head?" Anthony squealed with delight.

"Yeah, she was so fed up with him being out every night bowling with his friends, that she's cut of his head and is going to use it as a bowling ball. That's her revenge!"

"Cool!"

"And when she gets a strike, she says something cool like Hasta La Vista baby"

That was the type of conversation we used to have, just letting our imaginations run wild as we made stuff up.

As an adult, I had completely forgotten how to do that. It was as if all the experience I'd crammed into my brain over the years had entirely crowded out my imagination. When I was with Anthony, however, I felt like a kid again. My little cousin had helped me re-discover my imagination.

For me, those Saturdays with Anthony were utterly refreshing. I'd reached a stage in my life which a lot of people my age get to, where you feel like you're just running to stand still. On weekdays I'd start off every morning full of optimism, but that would end as soon as I got to work and sat down at my desk. After that, it was as if I was just going through the motions. Spending time with Anthony, however, somehow rejuvenated me and it affected what I did during the week. I started to indulge my imagination more and found myself coming up with creative solutions. Without my realizing it, my little cousin's influence had quite literally revived me.

When Anthony was twelve, he won a place at a prestigious secondary school, Stephen's College in Stanley village, Hong Kong. On one of our last Saturday bus rides together, we went to visit the school. It was during the summer holidays before Anthony was due to start there, so we practically had the place to ourselves. There's a beautiful view from the school, overlooking the South China Sea, and as we stood there looking at the view, I glanced over at Anthony.

I saw that same look of resolution that I had seen on his face the day his father had died. But mixed in with it all this time was a sense of pride. Anthony knew that St Stephen's was a significant milestone towards achieving the silent promise he had made to his father. I saw him maturing from the child I knew into the well-rounded, strong-minded adult he was destined to become.

I also knew that St Stephens marked a turning point in our relationship. From then on I would see less of Anthony, as his own life took off. Take off it did. He threw himself into school activities and milked every experience for what it was worth. He would always be my little cousin, but I was proud of him as was his mum and we both knew his dad would have been proud of him too.

Life's random cruelty

I remember receiving the phone call when I had just come home from work. It came from one of his mum's Korean friends who had somehow found my number. I prayed she was wrong, that maybe something had got lost in translation and I had misunderstood what she was saying. But when I arrived at the hospital, the horrible truth was confirmed. A random bout of scarlet fever had taken Anthony, my young cousin, from this earth. He had passed away. He was fifteen years old.

Shock took me in its grasp, disbelief that this had happened. "Hows" and "whys" stumbled from my lips, but the answers hardly mattered, not now that Anthony was gone. What words of consolation could I offer his mother, who having lost her husband had now lost her wonderful son?

That was when the rage started to surge through me, sheer fury at the unfairness of it all. How badly I wanted to lash out at something, anything.

Then a moment of clarity, pierced my thoughts. A memory from nowhere, sparking through the red mist. The memory of how Anthony, an eight-year old boy, had reacted to his own father's death, that calm resolution he had shown, the vow he had made, that depth of character he had displayed.

Here, even though he was gone, Anthony was showing me how I should be reacting to his own passing. Here was a final reinforcing life lesson from my cousin, to go with all the other life lessons he had taught me along the way. He had, during his short life, reconnected me with the child-like imagination I once possessed. He had given me back a sense of fun, shown me the joy of the unexpected and how this could open up new horizons for me at my age, when I had already thought I had begun to plateau. All of this was the result of nothing more than spending quality time in each other's company on those bus-rides to nowhere.

It was then that I realised this relationship had a name. A name passed down from Greek mythology to denote someone who was a trusted friend and advisor, someone with great wisdom, who passed that wisdom on and nudged you on the right path to achieve your full potential.

Anthony had been my mentor, without either of us realizing it.

Being guided by youth

In the years following Anthony's passing, I found myself inspired by the lessons he had taught me. But it was a different sought of inspiration to anything I had previously known. This was not the kind of short-term boost you get from listening to a high-tempo song, like the training montage from Rocky III, or hearing a speech laced with uplifting rhetoric, or attending a training course on how to improve yourself; nor was it an inspiration that unleashed an unbridled sense of short-term joyful motivation, the type that wears out as soon as the immediate passion is gone. Rather, it was an inspiration that created a constant restlessness, a continual fidgeting to get what I needed to do done.

Anthony's inspiration served as a powerful driving force, precisely because of the obsessive quality it had let rip in me. I felt like a young man in a hurry again, only this time, with the onset of age, Anthony's lessons had emboldened me with a sense of urgency. It was inspiration that came from the head, not the heart and was built on the construction of logic I had learned, rather than a transient sense of passion.

Somehow, Anthony had reconnected me with the child-like curiosity I had once possessed. This curiosity had been eroded over of the years as I had developed my own opinions and experience which had squeezed it out of my being. Now, however, it was back and it was burning brightly. I again found myself questioning things like I had done as a kid. I began to ask "why" and "what if". Only now my curiosity was combined with the knowledge and ability to endure, which I had developed with age, so I was able to push myself to stay the course in finding answers.

So it came to be that I broke out of the complacency into which I had settled on reaching the cusp of middle-age. Indeed until the point I began to break free from it, I had not even recognized the complacency for what it was. I had mistaken it for a kind of contentment, the stage in life for which I had been striving all along, where the constant drive to improve could stop and I could finally start enjoying the fruits of my labour. This was, I thought, the end for which I had been working, where I no longer needed to push the boundaries. I could take a back seat and coast and fall back on the experience which I had spent years developing.

I was fooling myself, however. Relying on the experiences of the past had made me skeptical about anything new that came across my path. Over time, a conservatism had begun to grip my mind, tightening it to the point of rigidity in a vice of preconceived ideas and opinions and prejudices. I was intuitively fooling myself into thinking that the way we do things now must be preserved, taking on a misguided sense of superiority for the way things are and immediately reacting to any new idea with pointed questions aimed at denigrating it. The beginnings of a typical grumpy old man were developing in my soul. We all know the type of person I am talking about. They are the ones who spend their days reminiscing about "the good old days" as if it was some sort of golden age, harking back to simpler times and seeing nothing but wrong in the modern world and the youth of today. They are the ones who are resistant to any sort of change. I had joined their ranks.

What made this complacency, this conservatism, this mask of superiority all the more dangerous was how I had completely failed to see it and indeed was justifying it as the way it should be. It took Anthony's influence to lift the veil. He made me see that all I was doing was justifying the sloth into which my life had slipped. He made me realize that life's journey is not about reaching a pre-determined peak, like I thought I had reached. It is about a constant striving to find new peaks within yourself and building character through every challenge faced.

Life is not a linear journey to a fixed end of success. It is not about ticking boxes of things done just so you can look back and say you have done them. Life's path is about recognizing that we as individuals are made up of both strengths and weaknesses and as human beings we must continually struggle every day through every challenge presented and not let our weaknesses overcome us. By this struggle we push the boundaries of ourselves and find new hidden depths. We slowly but surely etch the values which we hold dear into our character. By doing this every day, every hour, every minute we gradually but surely move a step closer to making living by these values instinctive and intuitive, thereby becoming the best human beings we can be. It is not comfort we should be seeking in life. It is fulfillment and we should never stop.

It took the influence of an eight-year old to put me back on track, precisely because, unlike me, Anthony possessed none of the superiority which I had adopted in my complacent state. He was able to challenge and unsettle me in the way that I so desperately needed. He knocked me off balance.

The most manifest consequence of this unsettled inspiration was my journey to becoming a novelist. This was something I, like millions of others, had always wanted to do when I was younger, but the restless mind which Anthony's tutelage had somehow released, inspired me to achieve it. It was as if I was on those bus rides again with him, making up stories about the people we saw through the window, letting my imagination run wild. Only this time, when combined with the research skills, the techniques of analysis and planning I had learned in my day job and the ability to think in years (like people do as they get older) rather than just days, I was able to channel my creativity towards achievement. I was able to endure and make my creativity last longer.

It didn't stop with novel writing, however. Every piece of work I was given in my day job became an opportunity to learn rather than a piece of drudgery to see through to completion. Every chance that presented itself, I grabbed with both hands because I saw in it an opportunity for personal growth. This was how I started teaching part-time on the law course at the local university. This was how I came to speak in public twenty times in a single year. This was how I was still able to pick up lever arch files and scan the paper myself, rather than delegate it, because it helped me gain endurance and put me back in touch with the restless spirit I had as a young trainee lawyer who was eager to improve.

This sense of inspiration was by no means comfortable, but it was inspiration all the same, and it operated to drive me forward, where before the limits of my experience had restrained me. Somehow, Anthony's influence had broken me free from those restraints and allowed me, even compelled me, to channel my experience into new things and be creative and imaginative.

My complacent desire for comfort was replaced by a restless search for fulfilment. I felt there was work to do, that my work had purpose and that it was vital I do it to the best of my abilities. I felt I was constantly putting my character to the test, and if I came through those tests, my character improved.

After a few years of this, I found this child-like curiosity turning in on itself. I began to ask what had happened to me and how it had happened. How was it that a young kid like Anthony could hold the key to unlocking my experience from its constraints? How could one, so young, mentor someone two generations older than himself and have such a profound impact on his outlook to life?

I thought perhaps that Anthony leaving this world at such a young age was where the answer lay. That the reminder this served of the fragility of life, was the impetus behind my new-found drive to make the most of it. Although this may have provided a partial answer, it was by no means complete. There was something deeper at play here, a change in psyche which had begun to evolve in me from the time I spent with Anthony, rather than it being developed after his passing. The answer lay somewhere in that connection across the generations which Anthony and I had stumbled on.

The answer lay in the dynamic of reverse mentoring.

Chapter 4

THE ORIGINS OF REVERSING MENTORING

Mentoring questioned

The origins of mentoring are based on a quite astonishing misunderstanding.

The first recorded use of the word 'mentor' comes from Greek Mythology, in particular from Homer's epic poem the *Odyssey* about the adventures of Odysseus, King of Ithaca, and his dramatic journey home from the Trojan War. It is commonly believed that in the *Odyssey*, when Odysseus leaves his kingdom in search of adventure, he places one of his old friends in charge of bringing up his son, Telemachus. This friend's name is Mentor. Mentor, it is understood, plays a kind of father-substitute for Odysseus, serving as teacher, counsellor and role-model for the young Telemachus.

It is from Homer's Odyssean character, that the word "mentor" and our understanding of "mentoring" is derived; namely, a relationship in which an experienced trusted adviser – a mentor – counsels, nurtures and provides guidance to a younger protégé.

In his essay, "Homer's Mentor: Duties Fulfilled or Misconstrued",[1] Andy Roberts reveals an entirely different truth, however. Homer's Mentor was never the man we think he was. Mentor certainly appears in the *Odyssey* as an old friend of Odysseus to whom the King had entrusted his whole household when he left Ithaca. There is no mention, however, of Mentor ever being assigned any particular role in Telemachus' upbringing, still less that he offered Odysseus's young heir any guidance or education, or fulfilled any kind of mentoring role.

Rather, in the *Odyssey*, it is the Goddess Athena who serves as Odysseus's protector, providing guidance and counsel to both Odysseus and Telemachus. She does this through a process of inhabiting the minds of existing characters and animals and using them as vehicles through which to dispense her advice. Mentor is one of the forms she takes for this purpose, but this makes Mentor no different from any of the other vehicles Athena used, which include a seagull, a daughter of a ship's captain and a young shepherd. To the extent that anyone displayed any mentoring qualities in the *Odyssey*, it was Athena rather than Mentor. That it is Mentor and not Athena whose name has entered the English lexicon to define mentoring, serves perhaps as an early example of gender bias.

When Mentor was not being used as a vehicle through which to channel Athena, he appears not to have been doing very much at all in the *Odyssey*. He completely fails in his role as caretaker of the royal household, as Ithaca becomes overrun by spongers and suitors intent of frittering away the country's wealth in their endeavor to marry Penelope, Odysseus's wife, when it was assumed Odysseus was dead.

Why, then, is it Mentor and not Athena whose name has been adopted as part of the English language? The answer lies in a French publication written some three millennia after the *Odyssey*.

François de Salingac de La Mothe Fenelon, served as a tutor to Louis XIV's grandson, the Duke of Burgundy, in the late 17th and early 18th centuries. In 1699, Fenelon published *Les Adventures de Telemaque*, which imitated Homer's style and served as a continuation of the *Odyssey*.

Telemaque follows the adventures of Telemachus, using Telemachus to illustrate the ideals of enlightened monarchy in comparison to the unenlightened absolutism of Louis XIV. In this way, Telemaque serves as a hagiographic instruction manual on the duties of royalty for the young Duke, under Fenelon's tutelage. It is in

Telemaque that we suddenly see Mentor acquiring the role which has made his name famous, serving as a kind of second father to the young Telemachus, regulating the whole course of Telemachus' life, so as to enable him to attain his full potential. As such, it is thanks to Fenelon's 18th century re-interpretation of Mentor's role, that the character's name has entered into the English language to define mentoring.

So there it is: modern day mentoring is based on falsity. The old man who failed in his original role as a royal household caretaker is remembered for posterity by reason of his role being re-interpreted, some three thousand years later, by a French teacher from Burgundy.

I should have been disappointed by this discovery, but somehow it makes utter sense.

The role which Anthony, my younger cousin, had played in my life did not fit that of "wise old counsellor", which is the way we think of "mentoring'. Indeed, here is proof again, of the enduring bias which our society fosters in favour of experience and age at the expense of youth and creativity. Here is proof that the very concept of mentoring, and the assumptions on which it is based, are ripe to be challenged, re-thought and, most of all, reversed.

The origins of reverse mentoring

Jack Welch, the renowned Chief Executive General Electric Co., is credited with first coming up with the idea of reverse mentoring, when he required five hundred of his top-level executives to pair up with younger employees to learn how to use the Internet. This was the first known reverse-mentoring programme in the world, where members of the younger generation took on the role of mentor to senior executives in order to teach them new ways of doing things.

Within a decade of GE's pioneering programme, the corporate world had fully embraced the reverse mentoring concept, with senior management using the dynamic to stay up to date with technological advances and how to use social media. Both Cisco and Hewett Packard developed their own schemes, with younger employees offering advice to older managers on how to use Facebook and jazz up their Twitter posts.

The younger mentors in these programmes also benefited, as they gained exposure to senior management early on in their careers and found themselves able to ask questions about things in their companies that would otherwise have remained a mystery to them. This heightened level of transparency led, in some cases, to reduced turnover at the junior levels as it created a greater level of appreciation throughout the company of the strategic decisions being taken at the top of the house. With understanding came a greater sense of belonging, so the story goes. Further, the practice of reverse mentoring in the workplace gave senior management a means of keeping in touch with the grass roots, providing a channel for them to listen to and react to employee needs. It was, to use corporate speak, 'win-win' for both generations.

On the face of it, this makes a lot of sense. Yet, when I first discovered that the origins of reverse mentoring lay in the corporate world, I felt somewhat disappointed. True, it was clear that the business world was obtaining tangible benefits from its use, as senior management were being up-skilled and kept current in the latest technologies. To my mind, however, when you stripped away everything else, this up-skilling of senior executives was being achieved through the provision of free training from those in the lower levels at the company (an expense-savings scheme, really, when you think about it). The quid quo pro for the young mentors was higher visibility in the company and the path to faster career progression; or to use the proper no-nonsense description of it, "getting on by kissing ass".

In short, reverse mentoring appeared to me to be nothing more than a new management technique, which was in danger of becoming the type of short-term fad hi-jacked by those of a Machiavellean disposition looking to short-cut their way up the corporate ladder. No wonder I felt disappointed!

Despite all of this, there was one key aspect of corporate reverse mentoring which drew my admiration and that was the underlying challenge it presented to traditional mentoring. Here, after all, was the assumption that "you can only learn something worthwhile from someone older than you" being turned on its head. It was the casting out of this assumption that I was sure underpinned my relationship with Anthony as described in the previous chapter. I had learned from him. His eight-year old precocious mind had inspired and changed me.

The reverse mentoring dynamic which Anthony and I had stumbled on seemed to go so much deeper than its corporate version. It was not just a matter of pure knowledge transfer on the use social media. Anthony's influence had created an inherent change in my psyche. It had been life-changing and purpose-defining. Because of this, I felt the corporate version of reverse mentoring was hardly scratching the surface of what it could accomplish. This was no management-speak fad, and to treat it as such risked dismissing it as an irrelevance. Through personal experience I had discovered that reverse mentoring had the potential to be a life-changing dynamic, the power of which we had not even begun to discover. It was a subject crying out for further research, a potential gold nugget buried deep in the mud, which needed to be excavated.

That's exactly what I set out to do and this book is the result.

What did I find out? You will have to read on to find the full answer, but in short, what I discovered has blown me away. Probably my most interesting discovery is that reverse mentoring is not new at all. Rather, it has existed in different forms throughout the course of history. Indeed, some of the world's greatest leaders have benefited from its influence and, without even knowing it, have used it to fulfil accomplishments that have changed the world. Put simply, reverse mentoring has already been proven to have the power to inspire great things.

All we need to do now is find a way of harnessing that power to inspire ourselves.

Chapter 5

RECONNECTING WITH THE CHILD-LIKE MIND

On 15 October 1815, Napoleon Bonaparte stood on the deck of the HMS *Northumberland* and stared up at the forbidding cliff tops of St Helena. This volcanic island in the middle of nowhere was to be his home and prison for the rest of his life.

This time the British had taken no chances. Just over a year had passed since they had made the mistake of thinking Napoleon's first bout of exile on the little island of Elba off the coast of Italy, would be sufficient to confine him. It had turned out to be a costly decision, one which had underestimated the limits of Napoleon's indomitable spirit and incredible ability to turn his vaunted ambition into action. On 1 March 1815, fewer than ten months after being sent to Elba, Napoleon was back in France, landing near Cannes and marching north on the Route Napoleon, the name given to this famous journey through the Alps back to Paris and power.

On his march north, at the town of Laffrey, the Napoleonic legend was sealed once again. He encountered a battalion, readying to fire on him with muskets drawn. Napoleon stepped forward. Dramatically throwing off his grey cloak, he revealed his identity and dared them to shoot their Emperor. A single bullet at that moment could have changed the course of history. Instead the battalion threw down their arms and mobbed Napoleon with joyous cheers.

Napoleon went on to take the arsenal at Grenoble before continuing to Autun, Avallon and Auxerre, entering Paris on 20 March 1815. There, he took up residence at the Tuilleries, vacated in panic the previous day by the fat Louis XVIII. Napoleon was Emperor once again.

Napoleon had first acquired Imperial title ten years previously at his magnificent coronation on 2 December 1804. Ironically, his path to becoming Emperor had been an astonishing testament to the French Revolution, which had overthrown an ancient régime – where birthright dictated one's place in the social hierarchy – in favour of a system based on merit. Born in Ajaccio Corsica in 1769 into a family which could just about class itself as minor nobility, at ten-years-old Napoleon had been admitted to the Royal Military School of Brienne-le-Chateau, near Troyes in France. So began a military career that would drive his trajectory to fame and glory. As a major, he masterminded the ejection of the British from Toulon. At the age of twenty-four, he was made a general and led the Army of Italy to a series of victories over the First Coalition of European countries intent on reversing France's Revolution.

In 1798, he campaigned in Egypt, attempting to destroy the British trade routes to India. Successfully capturing that country, Napoleon fended off two Turkish invasions. But success in the Middle East was muted by naval defeat at the Battle of the Nile; failure to gain control of the seas proving to be Napoleon's ultimate Achilles' heel throughout his career. Nevertheless, Napoleon's Egyptian campaign made a lasting contribution to the intellectual advancement of Europe. French academics took the opportunity to document artefacts from the ancient world and returned home with a body of knowledge that would have a profound impact on the future of continental culture and architectural design.

In 1799, Napoleon was back in France as Britain, Russia and Austria joined forces against her in the Second Coalition. The failures of the French government under the First Directory created the opportunity for Napoleon to seize political power in the coup of 18 Brumaire. He was named as First Consul in the three-member consulate that served as the French government. Victory against the

Austrians at the Battle of Marengo in 1800 secured his political dominance.

The consequent peace allowed Napoleon breathing space to focus on domestic governance and implement a programme of reform so revolutionary and forward thinking that its impact still underpins much of French society today. He unified the multiple legal codes of the *ancien régime* into a single unified system of law, which applied to all citizens. The Code Napoleon, as it became known, was based on principles of equality before the law, the sanctity of contract, property rights and the abolition of arbitrary arrest. It established a civil law system, still followed today in many European countries. In education too Napoleon was truly revolutionary, introducing a national secondary education system based on public schools known as lycées, which offered a learning programme, designed to produce the administrators, technicians and soldiers needed to run France. Further, the efficient administration of his government saw infrastructure projects come to fruition that still stand in use today.

Ironic though it is, Napoleon as Emperor oversaw the embedding of the French Revolution's principles of equality over birthright, rationalism over religion and meritocracy over cronyism, into French society. Or perhaps, instead of viewing this as ironic, one might say that Napoleon's rise to Emperor marked him out as the best example of the Revolution's prime accomplishment: a society based purely on merit, enabling talent to rise to the very top.

Following Napoleon's coronation as Emperor in 1804, the European powers of Britain, Russia, Austria and Portugal joined forces in a Third Coalition to overthrow him. Napoleon responded by leading the Grande Armée to victory at Austerlitz in 1805, arguably the greatest victory of his career. At Austerlitz, Napoleon's strategic brilliance and intuitive feel for battle were in full display. He lured the enemy into attacking his right flank, thereby weakening their line at the centre. When the time was right, the French pulverized the enemy down the middle in a swift and decisive counter-attack.

Napoleon was to take to the battlefield again the following year, with Prussia's declaration of war and its alliance with Russia in the Fourth Coalition. At Jena, Napoleon defeated the Prussians with another flawlessly executed plan. The attritional Battle of Eylau in 1807 saw Napoleon snatch stale-mate from the jaws of defeat with the most audacious cavalry charge of the Napoleonic wars, throwing back the Russian cavalry against its own infantry. He went on to rout completely the Russians at the Battle of Friedland with a focused and concentrated effort of military force. Exhausted and defeated, both the Russians and Prussians came to the negotiation table. Peace was agreed with the Treaty of Tilsit in July 1807, Russia submitting to Napoleon's Continental System, a European-wide embargo against Britain, which aimed to strangle the British economy by denying her ability to trade with Europe.

Napoleon then turned his attention to the Iberian Peninsula. He invaded Portugal in late 1807 to damage British commercial interests. A year later, he invaded Spain to co-opt her fleet as a French asset and secure France's southern border. Although Napoleon was able to name his brother King of Spain in 1808, the Spanish annexation absorbed huge numbers of troops. Continual guerilla warfare and local uprisings led to it being termed, Napoleon's "Spanish ulcer", throughout the rest of his reign.

No sooner had Iberia been temporarily quelled, however, than it was the Austrians' turn to have another attempt at breaking the Napoleonic Empire. With the help of a huge subsidy from Britain, the Austrian archduke Charles declared war in 1809, on behalf of the Fifth Coalition. The two armies, numbering 300,000 combatants, came together at Wagram in July 1809, and after two days of fighting, Napoleon was the uncontested victor, sending the Austrians into retreat. Peace was made at the Treaty of Schönbrunn.

The following year, 1810, marked the high point of the Napoleonic Empire in terms of territorial extent. The France he ruled consisted of 130 *départements* and was linked with the kingdoms of Italy, Naples and Spain. In effect these were under his control, ruled as they were by his family members or specially-appointed personnel. Further, the treaties he had signed meant alliances, albeit fragile ones, with Russia, Austria, Prussia, Sweden and Denmark. Only Britain stood alone. All of this and Napoleon was only forty-one years-old.

It was Napoleon's Russian campaign in 1812 that proved to be his ultimate undoing. Suffering from the constraints of trade imposed on it by the Tilset Treaty, Russia was soon openly turning a blind eye to the British trading ships using the American flag to breach the Continental System designed to suffocate the island nation's trade. Tsar Alexander's refusal to stop trading with the British in line with the Tilset conditions, and his obvious preparations for war, led to Napoleon's fateful decision to invade Russia with an army of over half a million men in June 1812. It was the largest army ever raised in history to that point.

The Russians, however, continually frustrated Napoleon, refusing to engage his forces in his preferred set-piece battle. Instead, they retreated within Russian borders, drawing the French army ever further eastwards. As they did so, the Russians burned and destroyed crops in their own country, placing further pressure on the French and stretching their supply lines beyond their limits. Finally, in September 1812, Napoleon caught up with the Russian army at Borodino. What followed was one of the bloodiest single-day battles in European history. Napoleon was victorious in carrying the field, but victory was muted by the number of casualties suffered and the fact that the Russian army was able successfully to retreat.

The following week Napoleon entered Moscow, but the Russian army had continued its self-destruction tactics by burning the city and releasing all prisoners, thereby providing little respite to the French. Napoleon stayed in Moscow for a month, allowing his army to recover whilst he pondered his next move. He could have advanced further east to try to finish the job and take Tsar Alexander's court. He could have stayed in Moscow and ridden out the winter. But his fear of being stuck east of the Nieman river in the midst of a Russian winter led Napoleon to make the fateful decision to take his army back to France, a move which began in October 1812, just as the first flurries of snow were falling. Seeing Napoleon's move, the Russians took their chance and continually attacked his rear divisions as they withdrew on their long march west.

It was the brutality of the Russian weather that finally destroyed Napoleon's army, which lacked provisions anyway as the destruction reaped on their own lands by the Russians earlier that year began to pay dividends. In November 1812, the temperature dropped to minus thirty degrees. The last of the French forces, such as they were, re-crossed the Nieman to safety in December 1812. Of the original army of over half a million that Napoleon had led into Russia, only 120,000 half-starved frostbitten soldiers made it back.[2]

In Napoleon's absence, the British had defeated French forces in Spain at Vittoria in June 1813, leaving France's southern border dangerously exposed. This, coupled with the conjoining of the Sixth Coalition, meant Napoleon was now under significant pressure. Still he came out fighting, raising an army and marching into Germany to try to re-establish power there, winning victories at Lützen, Bautsen and Dresden in 1813. Unable to knock Prussia out of the

Coalition completely, however, Napoleon set-out his forces at Leipzig. This seemed like his last roll of the dice.

At Leipzig, the Coalition finally won the decisive victory over Napoleon which they had been searching for. Napoleon was no longer a force in Germany and he was forced to retreat back to France, with Coalition forces in hot pursuit. During the opening months of 1814, Napoleon fought a series of battles in the Champagne region which frustrated the Coalition's ability to finish him off. This led the Coalition to change its tactics from attempting to defeat Napoleon in the field, to keeping him occupied outside Paris, whilst they slipped in and took the capital city.

The Coalition marched on the capital in March 1814, whilst Napoleon was too far away to assist. Paris fell on 31 March 1814. Napoleon, who, up until that point, had still been winning victories wanted to fight on, but his generals had no appetite for civil war. So, on 5 April 1814, after being promised exile with lifetime sovereignty on the island of Elba, Napoleon abdicated.

Elba held Napoleon's attention for ten months, but the indecisive manner of his ousting continually rankled with him. It was only a matter of time before he would try to regain what, in his view, had not been taken from him on the battlefield, the only arena which mattered in his eyes. So to Cannes and his audacious march north back to Paris.

In the three months between his return to Paris in March 1815 and his final defeat, Napoleon's work ethic remained astonishing and accounted for several key public works in the city. But the Allied European powers could not allow it to last, and on 15 May, war was declared.

The Battle of Waterloo, which followed in June 1815, remains one of the most famous turning-points in world history. Napoleon had risen to power by the sheer force of his talent, work ethic and self-belief. Having lost power, he had possessed the sheer hubris to take it back. If he had won at Waterloo, Napoleon would have changed the course of the world. But, for whatever reason, at Waterloo

Napoleon's military genius finally deserted him. The battle was lost as much by reason of his costly misjudgments, as by the skill of the Duke of Wellington and the other commanders ranged against him. For Napoleon, it was finally over.

And so, back to the deck of HMS *Northumberland* in October 1815, and the start of his exile on St Helena, the sub-tropical volcanic island measuring sixteen by eight kilometres in the South Atlantic ocean. What must have been going through Napoleon's mind at that moment, as he stared up at those imposing black cliff-tops that were to be his prison? He, who had ruled the greatest European empire since Ancient Rome, who had fought sixty battles and been unsuccessful in only seven of them, who had parlayed with royalty, who was adored by the men serving under him, whose sheer energy and intellectual capacity had laid the foundations for modern France and the legal system in much of Europe today and who was to give his name to the age in which he lived. He, whose achievements were viewed as astonishing even in his own lifetime, was now to be confined on this rock and to ignominy for the rest of his days in an exile that would serve as a constant reminder of his ultimate failure.

How hard it must have been for a man like Napoleon, who, at forty-six years old, may have been past his prime for those days, but certainly had enough years of intellectual rigour and energy ahead of him, to have nothing to expend it on! In spite of contradictory outward appearances, it would be understandable if Napoleon was experiencing feelings of depression, regret and sheer hopelessness as he stared out from the deck,.

But Napoleon did not lapse into feelings of despair. During his first three months on St Helena, he discovered a child-like humour, which not only enabled him to adapt to his new surroundings, but triggered his intellectual curiosity once again. This bout of rejuvenation was made possible by the influence of a fourteen-year-old girl, with whom Napoleon developed a remarkable and entirely innocent friendship, in what must be one of the earliest examples of reverse-mentoring in history.

Napoleon's reverse-mentor

The house which the British government had allocated for Napoleon on St Helena was called Longwood. Situated on Deadwood Plateau, it used to be the residence of St Helena's Lieutenant Governor. On Napoleon's arrival, refurbishment of Longwood was still ongoing, so, in the interim three months, Napoleon and his entourage were offered residence at "The Briars", home of the East India Company's superintendent, William Balcombe, and his family.

On inspecting "The Briars", Napoleon found himself pleased enough and agreed to stay. Instead of returning to Jamestown for a tour, he decided he would wait whilst his rooms were being made ready and he took a seat at the dining-room table.

Neither William Balcombe nor his wife spoke much French, and so the task of entertaining Napoleon was left to Betsy, the Balcombe's second daughter. Unlike her parents, Betsy's French was passable.

Betsy was fourteen years old. Like all British schoolchildren at the time, she had been brought up to think of Napoleon as evil's purest manifestation. Indeed, it was the habit of British parents at the time to threaten their children with a visit from the ogre Napoleon, if they misbehaved. Now here was the very same ogre sitting opposite Betsy in her home, about to be her housemate!

On hearing Betsy's assertion that she spoke French, Napoleon proceeded to test this, by asking about her studies and exploring her knowledge of geography in a stern cross-examination.

"What is the capital of France?" he asked.

"Paris," Betsy replied.

"Of Italy?"

"Rome."

"Of Russia?"

"Petersburg now," said Betsy, "Moscow formerly."

At this answer, Napoleon turned abruptly fixed Betsy with his piercing eyes. "Qui l'a brûlé" he asked. "Who burned it?"

Such was the fierceness of his demeanour that Betsy felt all her initial fears about this man coming to fruition, so instead of speaking the truth, she stammered, "I don't know."

"You know very well, it was I who burned it!" Napoleon said with a half-chuckle.

"I believe, sir," Betsy replied, regaining some courage at the erstwhile Emperor's levity, "the Russians burned it to get rid of you."

After a moment of shocked silence, Napoleon roared laughter. And so was sealed the intriguing friendship between the deposed forty-six year old Emperor and his new-found fourteen year old friend.[3]

What made the relationship work was the fact that Betsy was able completely to abandon all her pre-conceived notions of Napoleon and treat him like any other visiting adult, with a mixture of curiosity and as an opportunity for fun. Even more intriguing was how Napoleon responded to this:

"His manner was so unaffectedly kind and amiable, that in a few days I felt perfectly at ease in his society, and looked upon him more as a companion of my own age, than as the mighty warrior at whose name, "the world grew pale," Betsy wrote in her memoirs some years later.[4]

Indeed, Napoleon seemed to respond in kind by re-lapsing to his youth, taking on the mind of someone of the same age whenever he was around Betsy. Together, they used to play puerile pranks on each other and other visitors. When put in the hands of the former Emperor of Europe, these japes often bordered the thin line between hilarity and downright cruelty.

One day a certain Miss Legg came to visit "The Briars" with the friend of a daughter, evidently curious to see Napoleon. When Betsy discovered that the daughter was terrified at the prospect of coming face-to-face with the man who, in her mind, was the fallen scourge who had carried out such dastardly deeds across Europe, she ran to the garden eager to fetch Napoleon. Seeing an opportunity for some cruel fun, Napoleon spiked his hair and wandered into the house, shaking his head and howling like a madman. This was enough to send the visiting daughter into terrified hysteria. She had to be taken home. Napoleon was almost crippled with laughter. Of course, he then tried the same trick on Betsy, but Betsy just stood there looking disapprovingly at him, unaffected by what he told her were the agonized cries of a barbarous Cossack, which he had encountered in his many battles.[5]

So familiar did Napoleon become with the Balcombe children, that they found themselves able to tell him things no one else would have dared. Betsy's brother, Alexander, used to sit on Napoleon's lap and play cards with him. One day, Alexander showed Napoleon one of the cards, which had on it a picture of an Indian Moghul, decked out in all his finery.

"See, Bony, this is you," Alexander said, calling Napoleon the nickname which for years the satirists in the British press had assigned him.

Of course, no-one had ever dared call Napoleon "Bony" to his face before, so he asked his interpreter to translate, which the translator proceeded to do, only far too literally, leaving Napoleon confused regarding why the British public thought he was skinny and boney.[6]

Betsy outdid her brother when Napoleon showed her one of his magisterial swords. She asked if she could handle it, a request to which Napoleon acceded. Betsy proceeded to unsheathe it and then chased Napoleon round the billiard room with it, eventually trapping him in a corner (something that no enemy had ever managed to do on the battlefield). Having pinned him down at sword point, Betsy told Napoleon to say his prayers, for she was going to kill him. Her older sister was furious with Betsy's antics, so Betsy quickly surrendered the sword and apologised. Instead of punishing her, however, Napoleon found the whole episode amusing and pinched her nose with mirth.[7]

Most famously of all (as the press got hold of the story), was the time when Betsy convinced Napoleon to play blind man's bluff. Betsy started off being blindfolded and, it seems, Napoleon really got into the game, tweaking her nose and then running off until she caught the perpetrator. Alas, the perpetrator she caught turned out to be her sister, so Napoleon forced her to continue to be the "blind man". The fast and furious fun was only interrupted by a visiting dignitary's arrival at the Briar's, his purpose to seek an audience with Napoleon.[8]

Certainly, it is clear that the sheer fun which Betsy Balcombe created for Napoleon during the first few months of his long exile enabled him to adapt to his new surroundings on St Helena. This curious reverse mentoring relationship, however, did so much more than get Napoleon over the initial depression that the prospect of his life-sentence on this obscure and remote island must have presented. Betsy's influence rejuvenated Napoleon and made him believe that there was indeed life after his ignominious fall from the great imperial heights which he had scaled. Further, Napoleon realized he still had important work to do and Betsy's influence energized him for this, his final and perhaps most vital of missions.

Historian of his life
To secure his place in history Napoleon knew he had to influence the writing of that history. The record he left of his life had to be strong enough to convince people of his side of the story. That he proved to be so successful in doing this lay in the extraordinary raw material which his

life's achievements had given him to work with, the considerable literary ability he had developed throughout his career and the sheer energy he put into the exercise.

Research commenced during his time staying at the Briars with the Balcombes. Every morning, sometimes from as early as 4am, Napoleon would take up his position in the grapery and work until breakfast time. When his hand got tired of making notes, he would switch to dictating to his secretary, Las Casas, who had been tasked with recording Napoleon's extraordinary life. Other than Las Casas, no one was allowed to disturb Napoleon once he had taken up this spot. No one, that is, except Betsy.

Betsy was often his sounding board, when he replayed his battles on the billiard table, particularly Waterloo, to see how he could have managed things better to obtain a different result. The "thoughtlessness of youth", as Betsy put it, coupled with her privileged position as an intimate of Napoleon, also often led Betsy to ask Napoleon straightforwardly about the most controversial of subjects, which no one else would have dared, such as his abandonment of his sick troops in hospital at Jaffa during his Egyptian campaign.[9] In responding to these queries, Napoleon would rehearse and refine his side of the story. If he could convince a young girl, he must have thought, he could convince the world with the record of his life which Las Casas was writing.

Of the abandonment of his sick soldiers at Jaffa, Napoleon recounted to Betsy the dreadful utilitarian calculation he had had to make. His doctors had told him that these men were too sick to move and ill beyond recovery. Few would be alive within the next twenty-four hours in all probability, he was informed. To take them with him would risk plague spreading throughout his entire army, without enhancing anyone's chances of recovery. To leave them there alive, however, would be to abandon them to the cruelty of the advancing enemy. Napoleon suggested that his doctors administer them all a fatal dose of opium, a suggestion which the medics refused. Their job was to save lives, not take them. The British, having learned of Napoleon's suggestion, made much of it to cultivate the "Napoleon as Ogre" myth in their propaganda. But as Betsy recounts it, Napoleon informed her that had he been in the same position as those soldiers, he would have desired his suggested outcome. Indeed, had his son been there, Napoleon told Betsy he would have ordered the same, a particularly poignant comment, given the age of the one he was addressing. Instead, however, given the refusal of his medical men, Napoleon ordered the rear guard to stay with the ill soldiers until nature had taken its course and disease finally took them all.[10]

Napoleon also talked openly with Betsy about the assassination attempts on him, admitting that he had ordered the execution of the Duke d'Enghien after one such attempt, but dispelling the myth that he wore armour under his clothes in constant fear that the assassin would get him. He recounted how he had dodged death from a fanatical sculptor once, by refusing to pose for him on the basis that sitting still in one position for so long was not a luxury he could afford with his workload.[11]

Betsy was also accorded insights on Napoleon's thinking on monumental subjects that gave a flavour of where his mind lay. She challenged him by observing that she had learned he did not believe in the existence of God. To this, Napoleon appears to have shown irritation responding, "You have been told an untruth; when you are wiser you will understand that no-one could doubt the existence of a God."[12] She was also treated to his contemplations on the history of great men, as he worked out his own place in their pantheon.

All of Napoleon's efforts resulted in the production of a four-volume memoir entitled *Le Mémorial de Sainte-Hélène*, which Las Casas waited after Napoleon's death to publish. Had it been one of Napoleon's battles, then the publication of *Le Mémorial* would probably have counted as one of his greatest victories, the one that cemented his place in history. It went on to become the greatest international bestseller of the 19th century. In death, as much in life, Napoleon had dictated the script of the world.

Le Mémorial, however, was not the end for Napoleon. So active and energetic was his mind that, after completing his work with Las Casas on *Le Mémorial*, he went on to dictate a 238-page volume of the life of Julius Caesar. The biography turned out to be of considerable historical worth, not only for Caesar, but also for Napoleon in the way he placed himself (and to this day continues to be placed) alongside the Roman Emperor as one of the most famous figures in history.

It is hard to say how much Napoleon owed to Betsy in this regard. What we do know, however, is that she came into his life at its lowest point, when a lapse into despair, depression and perhaps suicide would have been the obvious route for a man who had fallen from the greatest of heights and who placed personal honour above all else. Instead, Napoleon appears to have re-discovered his inner child through Betsy and, in this, the renewed vigour required to complete the final important task of his life.

A relationship of equality and an openness to an inquiring mind

What had really happened here? What was the dynamic behind the spark of this relationship, which serves as one of the earliest and most extraordinary examples of reverse-mentorship in history? What can we learn from it, to seek the same qualities for reverse mentoring today?

Primarily, we see in this relationship Betsy's influence in re-connecting Napoleon to the child-like mind he once had, and the true value this brought to bear.

Throughout our lives the acquisition of experience dictates our attitudes, opinions and thoughts, gradually making us more specialised and hence better at what we do. Napoleon's experience was perhaps the most astonishing of all. His military skill and brilliant generalship – which was tested, developed and sharpened through the large number of battles that he fought and won – make him today arguably the most brilliant commander of all time. Further, no one can touch him when it comes to his meritocratic rise from Corsican minor nobility to head of the largest empire since ancient Rome. Yet, even in the case of Napoleon, we see how this experience had closed his thinking, leading to the *hubris* which made him believe he could win back his Empire in perpetuity, after losing it the first time, when he could instead have simply settled back and enjoyed lifetime sovereignty on the comfortable island of Elba.

In short, Napoleon's own experience led to his convincing himself of his own invincibility. He believed his own propaganda, and one might say, this, as much as anything else, led to his ultimate downfall.

His encounter with Betsy offered him the release from this hubris which had enclosed his mind. It gave him the freedom to caste off from Planet Napoleon and revert to the child he had once been. In so doing, Napoleon rediscovered the joy of youth and irresponsibility. We see this in the way he threw himself into the experience of playing blind-man's bluff and the sheer delight he took in the way Betsy cornered him in the billiard room with his own sword. This, from the man who had once thought of himself as invincible. In these childish antics, we see Betsy perhaps introducing Napoleon to a much-needed dose of humility, coupled with the obvious playfulness he was enjoying.

Betsy's influence therefore not only re-energised Napoleon, but made him remove his arrogant blinkers. With the removal of these blinkers, Napoleon realised he could not rest on his many laurels, that his legacy was not a foregone conclusion, that he still had work to do. It was this influence, perhaps, which led Napoleon to harness his energy to dictate his incredible experiences to Las Casas, which led to the publication of *Le Mémorial*. Producing this definitive record of his life was not simply a way of passing the time on St Helena. Rather, it was his attempt at final and everlasting victory. A victory he accomplished because of the sheer energy he threw into the task, making *Le Mémorial* the greatest bestseller of the 19th century. Behind this victory – the securing of his legacy for posterity – lay the combination of his own experience with the rejuvenation created by the reverse mentoring given to him by Betsy Balcombe.

Secondly, we learn from this relationship, how reverse mentoring works. Reverse mentoring is not simply about putting an older person of experience together with a younger person of no experience. If it was, then every parent-child relationship could be classed as reverse mentoring. The difference, however, is the equality that underpins reverse mentoring. Equality of attitude, as much as the difference in age, is a vital ingredient.

This is why the parent-child relationship does not lend itself to reverse mentorship, because to achieve equality it needs the older mentee to throw off all attitudes of superiority and expectations of respect that society often associates with age. This is particularly the case when it comes to parents and children. Yet, with Betsy, Napoleon managed to achieve it. Indeed, this was something Betsy herself noted.

> "I never knew him lose his temper or fall back upon his rank or age, to shield himself from the consequences of his own familiarity, or of his indulgence to me. I looked upon him, indeed when with him, almost as a brother or companion of my own age, and all the cautions I received, and my own resolutions to treat him with more respect and formality, were put to flight the moment I came within the influence of his arch smile and laugh."[13]

Reverse mentoring works because both parties in the relationship throw away society's preconceptions and accept that, between them at least, the playing field is level. This leap is required more from the senior person in age than the junior, but somehow the greater the age difference, the easier it is for the senior person to make the leap. Again, we see this observation made by Betsy herself:

"....this is particularly the case in the association of a person of mature age with very young people. There is generally a confiding candour and openness about them which invites confidence in return, and which tempts a man of the world to throw off the iron mask of reserve and caution, and to assume once more the simplicity of a little child."[14]

Equality then is the key. For it enables the youth to ask questions without any fear whatsoever and the senior to answer them candidly, without putting on the veneer of respectability that society demands which often hides the truth. We see the results of this, particularly in the way Betsy was able to cover ground with Napoleon that others thought were off-limits (the abandonment of his sick troops at Jaffa and her straight-out question regarding his perceived atheism, being cases in point).

But most of all, we see the results of this in the way Napoleon is perceived today. No leader, other than Churchill, has so single-handedly been able to dictate the course of his legacy for posterity, through the power of the written word. This, of course, is due mostly to Napoleon's remarkable achievements. But the debt he owes to his reverse-mentor, Betsy Balcombe, for her influence on him during the lowest point in his life in the first few months on St Helena, can never be discounted.

Chapter 6

THE JUDGE AND THE BOOKWORM

The Supreme Court of the United States is an exceptional institution. Its judgments decide important points of constitutional law which often shepherd in historic change, guiding humanity along the pathway to improvement.

The Court also provides a record for how society's attitudes and values change overtime. Change is often evolutionary rather than revolutionary. A decision rendered in one era can eventually, decades later sometimes, be rejected to reflect the changes wrought by societal attitudes. In 1857, for example, the Supreme Court held slaves to be property and not capable of citizenship in the infamous Dred Scott case.[15] In 1896, it went on to uphold the "separate but equal" doctrine in Plessy v. Ferguson, providing the legal basis for segregation.[16] Sixty years later, however, in Brown v Board of Education of Topeka (1954), the Supreme Court unanimously discarded "separate but equal", ending segregation as a matter of law and handing the civil rights movement the most important legal victory in its history.[17]

The nine Justices on the Supreme Court are appointed for life. Cases are decided by majority and it is open to the Justices to voice their dissent by writing minority opinions. Dissenting opinions trace the evolution of the conversation through the ages and, in some cases, change its eventual direction by offering up threads out of which a rich tapestry may be woven by a majority judgment in later years. In this respect, dissenting opinions can represent defeat in battle on the path to ultimate victory in the war of ideas.

One of the most famous dissenting opinions of all time was given by Justice Oliver Wendell Holmes Jr, in the case of *Abrams v United States 1919*.[18] It addressed the issue of freedom of speech as guaranteed by the Constitution's First Amendment and, to this day, stands as a statement that underpins that most vital of rights.

Holmes's opinion in *Abrams v. United States* grounded the necessity of the right to free speech in human fallibility. History shows us how the opinions that one generation has held as true are often discarded as being wrong by the next. Given this, we can never be sure that we are ever entirely right. The only way for us to have confidence in the opinions and ideas we voice, therefore, is to allow free rein for them to be challenged, so that every argument and alternative viewpoint is given opportunity to be put forward. As Holmes put it, progress can best be achieved by the "free trade in ideas", where "the best test of truth is the power of the thought to get itself accepted in the competition of the market."[19]

Holmes's "free trade in ideas" metaphor changed history, eventually emerging as the majority viewpoint in cases heard by the Supreme Court in the 1940s. Yet the concept goes far beyond free speech and underpins the case for diversity and inclusion more generally, which business, and indeed society as a whole, is currently adopting.

That Holmes wrote his *Abrams* opinion at the age of seventy-eight, near the end of his long and distinguished legal career, makes it all the more remarkable, and history has rightly accorded him the position of hero to civil libertarians. The truth, however, is more intriguing. For, unlike his fellow Justice on the court, Louis Brandeis, prior to *Abrams v United States*, Holmes was no champion of free speech. In the years leading up to the *Abrams* case, he had sided with the majority on many cases, in upholding censorship in the name of national security.

What prompted Holmes, nearing the end of the eighth decade of life, to change his mind? The seeds of this answer lie in the dynamic of reverse mentoring and the impact it had on the great Justice's thinking.

The restless intellectualism of a youthful bookworm

Holmes's personal conversion, from conservative proponent to author of one the great liberal statements of all time, is brilliantly told by Thomas Healy in his book, *The Great Dissent*,[20] a must read for any budding law student or anyone interested in the interplay between a judge's personal outlook and how this influences the development of jurisprudence. Healy tells the tale of how in the years leading up to *Abrams v United States*, Holmes – through a series of encounters with men like Judge Learned Hand, Zechariah Chafee and Felix Frankfurter – was persuaded to change his mind. Of all the people involved in this process of intellectual transformation, however, none was more instrumental in shaping Holmes's thoughts than Harold Laski.

Harold Laski had been born and brought up in Manchester, England. His sharp intellectual abilities were recognized early, winning him a place in New College, Oxford where he studied history. In 1916, Laski relocated to the United States where he lectured at both McGill and Harvard University and wrote for the New Republic. At this stage in his academic career, Laski was the very picture of a restless intellectual, prolific in his publications, controversial in his views, keen to make an impact on the world and to rub shoulders with people that mattered. It was this last character trait which led Laski to beg his friend and colleague, Felix Frankfurter for an introduction to Supreme Court Justice Oliver Wendell Holmes Jr.

The introduction took place in 1916 during a visit to Beverly Farms, Holmes's holiday getaway outside Boston when the Supreme Court was out of session. Holmes was seventy-seven years old at the time, Laski only twenty-four, but despite the five-decade age gap, the intellectual attraction was immediate, and thereafter, Laski became a frequent visitor and correspondent with the Justice.

They made an incongruous pair; Holmes, the venerable, tall and aristocratic civil war veteran, born of New England blue blood and nearing the end of his stellar legal career; Laski, the merchant's son from Manchester, grammar-school educated, slight in stature and with the restless hunger of a young academic keen to obtain recognition for his passionately held theories. Yet there was more than just background, generation and physique to separate them. They had very different political views: Holmes was a life-long Republican and Laski was a recent student militant who would later go on to become one of the most prominent socialist thinkers in Britain and chairman of the British Labour Party. In short, as characters, they could not have been more different. Yet they were drawn together by two special ingredients which all successful reverse mentorships acquire: a sense of equality and mutual respect.

Holmes, although superior in social status, career achievement and age, never allowed that superiority to become part of his exchanges with Laski, nor did he ever disdain Laski for his idealism, albeit he did not share it himself. He saw in Laski a young man of considerable intellect and relished the challenge presented by their exchanges, savouring the stimulation of thought they provided. Indeed, in Laski, Holmes recognized something of himself from his own youth, a passion in the beliefs he held and a lack of fear to question the status quo. Their exchanges enabled Holmes to recapture part of that for himself, keeping his own mind and experience fresh and exercised.

For a young academic of Laski's ambition, there was nothing more beneficial to assist his social climbing than establishing a close relationship with a sitting Supreme Court Justice. Yet to see this as Laski's primary motivation would be wrong. Laski was always considerate in his exchanges with Holmes, even in disagreement, a signal of the genuine respect in which he held the septuagenarian lawyer. Yet the fact that he was never afraid to engage Holmes in intellectual sparring, albeit usually with subtle strategies, demonstrated that an equality existed in their exchanges.

At this stage of his career, Laski's main focus was in promoting his theory of pluralism, the notion that society's progress was achieved through a variety of institutions, not just the state which certainly had no pre-eminent status to command people's exclusive loyalty. Yet within this theory lay a commitment to free speech, for its success rested on people's openness to debate the diverse ideas propagated by whichever institution to which they showed allegiance. From such discussions, social progress would emerge, he believed.

Laski also had an edge over Holmes in terms of his expanse of reading. His work as an academic, together with his role as book reviewer for the *New Republic*, made Laski a typical book-worm. This, coupled with his prodigious memory, meant he was able to call on obscure facts from a variety of sources to meet any contrary argument.

It was by suggesting reading material for Holmes, that Laski embarked on his sustained campaign to change the Justice's mind on the issue of free speech. During a visit to Holmes in 1918, when the conversation eventually turned to the issue, Laski produced a book he had discovered during his research on pluralism and suggested that Holmes add it to his reading list. The book was called *The Theory of Toleration under the Later Stuarts*.[21] It was written by Cambridge academic AA Seaton and, as its name suggests, seemingly had nothing to do with free speech. Rather, Seaton's focus was the struggle for religious freedom in 17th century England.

This was a classic Laskian flanking tactic in his intellectual conflict with Holmes. Laski was lulling Holmes into a false sense of security with the offer of a book that ostensibly had little to do with the subject matter Laski truly wanted to address. Yet the theory of religious toleration which Seaton's book espoused was entirely transferrable to the subject of free speech, and Laski knew it would catch the Justice's attention.

Seaton, in essence, concluded that toleration, in this case religious toleration, set the optimal conditions for human progress. Persecution, where one religious faith dominates and tries to eliminate all others, had been tried and had failed, serving only to waste society's energy in cultivating resentment. Further, persecution was grounded on a false premise, namely complete certainty of the persecutor's religion being the true religion and all other religions being wrong. No religion, however, could claim such certainty, the reason being that every religion is grounded on the concept of faith.

Faith in religion was necessary precisely because each religion accepts that, as human beings, we possess incomplete knowledge of the ultimate truth. We are thereby fallible and hence must have faith about things which are beyond the realm of our worldly knowledge. This combination of fallibility and incomplete knowledge, which makes faith necessary, means that, whilst faith in one's own religion is justified, there is no right to suggest that another person's religion is wrong and should be suppressed. Tolerance of, and co-existence with, other religions is therefore only logical.

Seaton, however, went even further by suggesting that toleration was not merely logical, but served a positive role in social progression. Religious faith, after all, was grounded on the natural human craving to search for the ultimate truth. Through toleration, one reached a position where multiple religions across all societies would engage in this search, coming at it from different angles and thereby enhancing the collective knowledge of all. Toleration, in other words, is an enabler for positive human progress.

What Seaton left unstated was, that what was true in the realm of religion, was also true in the realm of ideas and opinions. Laski, however, was confident that Holmes would draw the link for himself. When Holmes returned the book this confidence proved justified. The Justice liked the suggestion of even the humblest ideas contributing to the search for truth, and told Laski so.

With this success elicited, Laski continued to submit reading suggestions and Holmes recorded his thoughts on each book in letters to Laski. Some he liked, others he disagreed with, or thought of as progressive drivel. But he read everything Laski suggested and, in so doing, their intellectual bond strengthened.

The other book that Laski suggested, which had the most influence on Holmes's thinking, was John Stuart Mill's *On Liberty*.[22] Mill's essay was a classic. To this day it is regarded as one of the greatest statements of political philosophy ever written. Holmes had read it years previously, but at Laski's suggestion he took it up again.

On Liberty addresses the limits of power which government should legitimately be able to exercise over the individual. Mill's theory was based on the principle of harm, namely that the restriction of an individual's liberty by government was only justified in order to prevent harm to others. Mill specifically applied this principle to the issue of freedom of thought and discussion. As with Seaton, Mill based his argument for free speech on human fallibility. Suppression of other opinions can only be countenanced, if we are confident our own opinion is one hundred percent correct. But history demonstrates that the opinions of humans are entirely fallible. Society used to burn people because it thought them to be witches. The passage of time, however, showed that opinion to be nonsense. What was to suggest that the opinions we hold today would not be roundly proven to be false by future generations? Nothing, ergo our opinions are fallible.

By accepting the fallibility of our opinions, we also had to accept that suppressing opposing opinions was wrong, unless those opinions threatened harm to others. Yet Mill went further than this, accepting that, even though our opinions are fallible, we are still entitled to, and indeed have to act on them. Society, after all, has to function and acting on the beliefs and ideas we hold is vital for that to happen. This begged the question as to how we could justify acting on our opinions given that we had to accept their fallibility?

According to Mill, it was precisely because we had to have the confidence to act on opinions which are inherently fallible, that freedom of speech and thought was needed. For it is only by opening our opinions up to challenge, through free speech, that we can subject them to test and thereby place confidence in their credibility. In a world of free speech, every time an individual voiced an opinion he was preparing to act on, he did so with an unstated invitation for that opinion to be challenged and disproved. The truth of an opinion gained confidence in its credibility precisely because it was open to be challenged by other opinions, and it is that which gives us confidence to act.

Holmes saw the attraction in Mill's argument and, having allowed Laski to draw it to his attention, let it circulate round his thought processes and slowly take root.

So near, but yet still so far to go

When Holmes returned to start the new term of the Supreme Court in January 1919, he and his fellow Justices were immediately faced with three free speech cases. First up, was Schenck v United States.[23] Charles Schenck and Elizabeth Baier were Socialist Party members from Philadelphia who had been successfully prosecuted under the Espionage Act for publishing a leaflet opposing the draft for army service during World War I. Second up was an appeal by Jacob Frohwerk, the editor of a German language newspaper found guilty of violating the Espionage Act, for an editorial expressing sympathy with those who were subject to the draft, even though it stated they should comply with it.[24] Third up was an appeal by Eugene Victor Debs, the leader of the National Socialist

Party and a passionate orator who had electrified an audience in Canton, Ohio with a speech brimming with Marxist vitriol against the capitalist fat cats who had led the country into a war which the workers were now being forced to fight through the compulsory draft.[25] Debs had been careful not to call on anyone to dodge the draft, but a jury had nonetheless convicted him under the Espionage Act.

After hearing the submissions of all parties, the nine Supreme Court Justices got together to deliberate and it soon became clear that the majority (including Holmes) were in favour of affirming the convictions. Holmes, being the second most senior Justice on the Court, was assigned to write the majority opinion. He began with Schenck. Being first up, Holmes used Schenck to state the test which needed to be applied when considering issues of free speech and we see just how far down the road Laski's reading material had taken him.

Holmes started off with the question of whether the First Amendment, which required that Congress shall make no law abridging freedom of speech, was absolute. In other words, did the First Amendment require there to be no limits whatsoever placed on freedom of speech. In this, Holmes was clear, the answer was no. The right to free speech would not, for example, "protect a man in falsely shouting fire in a theatre and causing a panic".[26] In this phrase, the influence of Laski's reading list is clear, for we see John Stuart Mill's "harm-principle" made real for readers by means of an understandable analogy so typical of Holmes.

The next question – the million dollar question – was where to draw the line. It is here we see Holmes at his most judicial brilliant, adopting a formula of words that has moved smoothly into the English language lexicon.

Taking Mill's harm-principle as his basis, Holmes developed a test regarding where the boundaries of free speech would lie. "The question in every case is whether the words used are used in such circumstances and are of such a nature as to create a clear and present danger that they will bring about the substantive evils that Congress has a right to prevent."[27]

This "clear and present danger" formula expanded the limits of free speech beyond where they lay at the time. The possibility that speech might cause harm was replaced with the requirement that the danger harm must be "clear and present", i.e. probable and imminent.

Yet with Schenck, Frohwerk and Debs this proved to be a case of "so near but still yet so far", for Holmes. For having formulated the "clear and present danger" test, Holmes failed to apply it to the facts before him. Instead he asserted, that when a nation is at war (as it was, being at the time engaged in the First World War) and its citizens were being sent to fight, publications found acceptable in peace time were justifiably censored in war time. Holmes, in other words, had formulated a test which represented a surgeon's scalpel but had laid it down in favour of a baseball bat to justify the Supreme Court's majority decision.

The personal ingredient

Being "objective" and "reasonable" are part of any lawyer's skill-set. Legal professionals are drilled to be objective and unbiased in their advice. They ask not whether their client has done the right thing, but what a hypothetical reasonable person in the position of their client would have done. A step-by-step approach to finding out the pertinent facts of a case, identifying the relevant law and then applying the facts to the law to reach a conclusion, is how the legal mind works. Personal feelings don't come into it.

Lawyers who spend years working with a client in preparing a case for trial, getting to know them as an individual, all the while have to maintain an objective distance. This is a struggle, but it is a necessary part of any decent legal professional's toolkit.

Judges, by contrast, have an easier task, especially Supreme Court Judges who do not even have to hear from the litigants whose cases they decide, only the dry submissions of their lawyers. To them, the men and women whose fates lie in their hands, remain but names on a page. The law can be, in this respect, a very impersonal business.

Sometimes, however, the stars align to bring the events in a Justice's private life so near to an issue which lies before him in court, that it cannot help but have an effect on his thinking. When that happens, whilst objectivity remains, the personal elements sharpen rather than detract from the analysis and the result is all the more powerful. Such is what happened for Oliver Wendell Holmes when faced with the case of *Abrams v United States*.

Jacob Abrams was the leader of a group of Russian Jews who had distributed leaflets in New York calling for a general strike by workers at weapons manufacturers to stop producing materials for United States troops being sent to intervene against Russia a year after the Russian revolution. Abrams and his fellow anarchists were convicted under the Espionage Act for inciting resistance to the war effort against Germany, even though preventing the US from intervening against Russia had been their obvious intent. The leaflets themselves pointed out that Russia had done more than any other country in the fight against the Germans. Nevertheless they were convicted, as it was foreseen that a general strike in munitions would have a knock-on effect on the country's ability to meet the German threat.

Abrams and his colleagues appealed to the Supreme Court on the grounds that the convictions violated the First Amendment's guarantee of free speech. The case came before the Court in the autumn of 1919.

That same year, in a completely unrelated incident, the Boston police force went on strike to try to improve their working conditions. Public opinion turned vehemently against their actions, however, and the city commissioner used this to fire all who had participated in strike action. Only one person, it seemed, was prepared to speak up on behalf of the policemen. A young Harvard academic who had published a book arguing in favour of labour unions as a means of protecting the rights of workers. His name was Harold Laski, the young friend of Oliver Wendell Holmes. Jr.

In the same month that the *Abrams* case fell to be decided by the Supreme Court, Laski was quoted in the *Harvard Crimson*, supporting every Boston policeman's right to join a union and blaming the strike on the municipal authorities for failing to heed their grievances. Laski doubled down on these comments, by addressing a meeting of wives, sisters and mothers of the affected policemen, criticizing the city commissioner for his intransigence.

Laski's remarks immediately sparked a backlash, which threatened to end his Harvard career. Parents of students and Harvard alumni wrote to the President of Harvard, A. Lawrence Lowell, accusing Laski of Bolshevism and demanding his removal from the teaching faculty. The pressure on Lowell was significant, especially as Harvard itself was in the midst of a fund-raising campaign. A jealous guardian of academic freedom, however, Lowell refused to buckle. Even so, the board of Harvard agreed to discuss the issue at its next meeting.

Two days prior to the Harvard board meeting, at which Laski's fate was on the agenda, the Supreme Court Justices met to discuss their views in the case of *Abrams v United States*. Seven of the Justices were steadfast in their view that the convictions should be upheld. Unsurprisingly, Louis Brandeis disagreed. Holmes also voiced his concerns, particularly as it was clear none of the appellants had intended to hinder the war against Germany, merely to prevent intervention in the Russian Revolution. The majority of seven was enough, however, to decide the case. If Holmes or Brandeis wished to record their disagreement by way of dissenting opinion, it was up to their discretion.

At home that same evening, Holmes sat down to read a letter he had received from his friend Harold Laski. Holmes had already heard about the controversies into which Laski had become embroiled and, even though he disagreed with Laski's views, he sympathized with his friend's right to hold them and not have it affect his Harvard career. In Laski's letter and in Holmes's response, we see something quite remarkable happen.

We have already observed the complete deference to objectivity and reason that is part of a lawyer's skill-set, but there is another trait common to both the legal and academic professions worth noting at this juncture. The ability to write something which says one thing, but actually contains a meaning which is quite different. This is exactly what we see in the exchange of letters between Laski and Holmes at this moment in history.

Felix Frankfurter, a friend of Laski's and the man who had introduced him to Holmes, had been busy lobbying one of the Harvard trustees on Laski's behalf (the board being due to meet to decide Laski's fate in a couple of days). The trustee was the editor of the *Atlantic Monthly* and he had agreed to publish an article defending tolerance of free speech, in support of Laski and academic freedom, if Frankfurter or Laski could find a figure of authority to write it.

In Laski's letter to Holmes, Laski stated how it was a shame that Holmes himself could not take up this offer.[28] This suggested that either Holmes had already been asked and had refused, or that if asked, Holmes would refuse. What the sentence failed to do, however, was simply ask Holmes if he could write the article. But that is precisely what Laski – in his deferential, polite, academic and, yes, British way – was asking.

Holmes fully appreciated this, and that evening, he wrote a reply in which, for the first time, he claimed that the theory of free speech was one for which he would die.[29] Curiously, however, Holmes ended the letter apologizing (even though he had not been asked) for not being able to write the piece Laski was requesting, because he could spare no time to write anything outside of his legal duties.

As with Laski's hidden request, however, Holmes's response contained a hidden meaning, which not even Laski himself would have been able to elicit. Primarily, we see in the letter that Holmes's conversion to free speech, the result of a long period of influence from Laski and others, had now been made complete. This was precisely because, with Laski in trouble, the issue was no longer an abstract one involving people Holmes did not know. It was now very real and very personal.

Secondly, it was true, as Holmes stated, that he could not spare the time to write a defence of toleration for a magazine, as he was unable to write anything outside of his current legal duties. What Holmes left unstated, however, was that he was about to put pen to paper on something which would address the issue of toleration of free speech which fell directly within the core remit of his legal duties. It was in this frame of mind that the very next day Oliver Wendell Holmes sat down to write his dissenting opinion in *Abrams v United States*.

We can see in Holmes's opinion in *Abrams v United States*, the synthesis of the influence brought to bear by Laski's reading list and Holmes's own considerable legal experience. This synthesis makes the opinion a perfect example of the results which reverse mentoring can achieve.

Holmes begins with an argument reminiscent of Seaton (the author introduced by Laski), justifying toleration on the grounds of the fallibility of the opinions we hold, history showing us how "fighting faiths" believed to be true in the past, had subsequently been set aside as false by later generations.[30] Next, Holmes addresses the limits to free speech, embracing John Stuart Mill's harm-principle. Given the fallibility of opinions, it is logical that toleration and the ability to voice any idea should be permitted at all times, unless the voicing of the idea prompts an imminent threat of immediate harm.

It is with the third aspect of Holmes's free-speech defence in *Abrams v United States*, however, where we see the magic happen. Holmes was convinced by Mill's justification that the only way we can be confident in our opinions is to subject them to challenge by all. Holmes, however, wanted to put this into a frame of words which the general population would take to heart. Even though Laski had presented him with the path to Mill, it was only when Holmes mixed in his own experience as a Republican who believed in free market competition, that his *Abrams* opinion transitioned from a treatise of law, into an accessible statement of values which has stood the test of time.

"….the ultimate good desired is better reached by the free trade in ideas – that the best test of truth is the power of the thought to get itself accepted in the competition of the market, and that truth is the only ground upon which their wishes safely can be carried out."[31]

The free trade in ideas

So was born the notion of the "free trade in ideas", the concept that toleration, diversity of thought and the inclusiveness to have those thoughts heard, provides the pathway to truth and human progress. Reading Holmes's words now still makes the blood rush and the heart beat faster, such is their power. The magic of his analogy is as relevant today as it ever was.

Indeed, Holmes's dissenting opinion perhaps serves as the best example of that notion, for it emerged from the free trade in ideas between a seventy-eight year old judge and a bookworm academic called Harold Laski some fifty years his junior. In itself, this relationship makes the opinion all the more remarkable and offers us a powerful illustration of exactly what reverse mentoring can achieve.

Chapter 7

THE CATALYST FOR CHANGE

The 28th of August 1963 was a momentous day in American history. A quarter of a million people gathered in the nation's capital for the March on Washington for Jobs and Freedom. It was the largest demonstration of its kind, a moment in society when a tipping point had been reached. Martin Luther King, Jr. stood in front of the Lincoln Memorial to address the massive crowd, declaring "I have a dream", lifting the art of oratory to a new high. The gathered masses stood as one to swear an oath demanding racial equality. The March served as the catalyst for Lyndon B. Johnson (then vice-president, but later president) to push through the Civil Rights Act in 1964 to end segregation across the South, giving human dignity the full backing of the law.

History tells us that the March came about because for a single day, the six major civil rights organizations and their respective leaders were able to put aside their differing agendas and methods of action and come together as one. The "Big Six" as they were known were James Farmer of the Congress of Racial Equality (CORE), Martin Luther King Jr of the Southern Christian Leadership Conference (SCLC), John Lewis of the Students for the Nonviolent Coordinating Committee (SNCC), A. Philip Randolph of the Brotherhood of Sleeping-car Porters, Roy Wilkins of the National Association for the Advancement of Colored People (NAACP), and Whitney Young, Jr. of the National Urban League.

Whilst these six have been credited as the key organizers of the March, one of their number certainly stands head and shoulders above the rest in terms of his contribution. Philip Randolph was in his seventies at the time and already a respected doyen of the civil rights movement. The 1963 march was the manifestation of an idea he had first conceived in 1941. Back then, Randolph had threatened President Roosevelt with a mass descent on Washington, unless Roosevelt ended segregation in the defense industry, which at the time was refusing to hire black workers, thereby preventing them serving their country in the Second World War. Randolph's brinkmanship forced Roosevelt's hand and Executive Order 8802 was issued, banning discrimination across all defence industries.

Fast forward twenty years to 1963 and another president, President Kennedy, was requesting Randolph to stop the march. This time Randolph refused and America had its moment.

Yet, even to single out Randolph alone as the March's main proponent is misleading. Rather, the key to the 1963 March lay in a mentoring partnership of which Randolph was just one piece. The other partner was a man twenty years Randolph's junior. His name was Bayard Rustin. The instrumental role Rustin played in bringing the 1963 March to fruition has almost been erased from history.[32] Yet, in Bayard Rustin's long association with Philip Randolph, we see the true dynamic of reverse mentoring and the power it has to change the world.

A born pacifist steeped in nonviolence

Bayard Rustin was born in Westchester Pennsylvania in 1912 and brought up by his grandmother Julia. Julia was a Quaker and the dominant influence on Bayard's early life. She taught Bayard lessons that would stay with him forever, including the need to present a calm demeanor to the outside world on all occasions. At school, Bayard was academically precocious, musically gifted and athletically excellent, leading his track team to numerous successes. It was in the realm of school athletics that he first encountered directly the deep-seated prejudices against

African Americans that existed in society. His Westchester school had one of the few integrated athletic squads in the country, and because of this, white coaches from other schools often refused to field their teams in the same competitions. This experience meant that even before Bayard left school, he formed a moral resolve not to accept the restrictions that white America sought to impose on his race.

After a brief stint in college, Bayard became involved with the pacifist movement, which was gaining ground in the 1930s as the rise of Fascism in Europe brought the prospect of militarism to the fore. Bayard's Quaker roots led him easily to find a place in the activist wing of pacifism, something he explored further on moving to Harlem in New York in 1937, then a hot bed of political radicalism. There, he taught English, flirted with a career on the stage and began his career as a political radical by joining the Young Communist League, observing that whenever blacks got into trouble in Harlem, it was the communists who stood up for them. His links with communism, however, ended in 1941 when the party's growing embrace of militarism came into conflict with his own pacifist beliefs.

Instead, Bayard Rustin found himself being recruited by AJ Muste to become a youth secretary for the Fellowship of Reconciliation (FOR), a Christian pacifist organization which aligned with his Quaker upbringing. Bayard's initial association with FOR came at a time when pacifism was at its lowest ebb in American society. The Japanese attack on Pearl Harbour had spread the widely-held view that the nation was involved in a just war. Nevertheless, as a member of FOR, Bayard Rustin wore his pacificist credentials on his sleeve. Indeed, he became heavily influenced by Gandhi's model of non-violence, which he saw as a means to achieving FOR's aims.

On his travels as a FOR activist, Bayard used Gandhian nonviolence to counter racial discrimination whenever he encountered it. He was furious about Christian-run prison camps for conscientious objectors in the South being racially segregated and he called on the prisoners to resist this. These experiences led Rustin to develop a belief in the power of nonviolence to eliminate injustices that went beyond the mere promotion of pacifism. FOR was also moving in the same ideological direction, and as a result of this impetus, the Congress of Racial Equality (CORE) was launched as an offshoot of FOR, marrying nonviolent resistance with the fight against racial oppression

The founding of CORE enabled FOR staff to dedicate themselves to the issue of race relations and Bayard Rustin threw himself into this effort. He became a one-man nonviolent army, adapting Gandhian non-violence to attack racism wherever he saw it. It was this experience which first brought Bayard to the attention of Philip Randolph, who at the time had just called off his proposed march on Washington after successfully forcing Roosevelt to desegregate the defence industry. Randolph was interested in using this momentum to push on with expanding African American civil rights, and saw in the tactic of nonviolent civil disobedience a means of taking things in a radically different and impactful direction. Randolph wanted to deploy nonviolence in a concerted effort to resist the segregation laws all across the South and he wanted Bayard Rustin's help in doing this.

Prisoner of conscience
In November 1943, however, Bayard Rustin received his draft papers. Staying true to the pacifist principles, he conscientiously objected. He was arrested in January 1944 and sentenced to three years imprisonment. So it was that Bayard's next mission presented itself: to desegregate the prison he was in. During the twenty-eight month period of his incarceration, Bayard was a thorn in the side of the Prison Bureau and, because of this, one of the most notorious offenders of the time (alongside Al Capone).

The Federal Prison at Ashland, Kentucky never knew what hit it when Bayard took up residence as one of its inmates. No sooner had he arrived than Bayard sent Robert Hagerman, the warden at Ashland a memo on how to end racial segregation in the prison. Practicing what he preached, Bayard refused to sit in the section designated for coloured inmates at the weekly movie viewing. He also taught classes to white inmates, some of whom came from poor backgrounds in the hill country of Tennessee, seeing this as a means of spreading progressive attitudes where they were most needed.

In one incident, Bayard was attacked by a white supremacist inmate with a wooden mop handle for being in a whites'-only space. When other inmates rushed to his defence, Bayard told them to stand back and he took the blows in a perfect display of nonviolent discipline. His attacker eventually stopped, entirely unnerved by Bayard's reaction. Bayard emerged with a broken wrist, but news of the incident spread and became folklore in the pacifist and civil rights movement. It also served as a catalyst to Bayard to petition warden Haggard again to end segregation at Ashland. This time Haggard agreed to move forward, providing an interracial section in the theatre and introducing interracial tables in the dining hall.

Just as it seemed Bayard was making headway, however, another form of prejudice stepped in to cut away his momentum, in what was to become a story repeated throughout his career and the reason why the name Bayard Rustin was almost erased from history. Bayard Rustin was a homosexual in a society where to be homosexual was a crime.

The prison authorities saw in Bayard's homosexuality the opportunity to curtail his activism. He was brought before the prison disciplinary board to face accusations that he had partaken in homosexual acts. His vehement denials were followed by six weeks in solitary confinement. During this time, Bayard was visited by AJ Muste, the leader of FOR. Eventually, Bayard confessed to Muste that he had indeed succumbed to his homosexual urges. Bayard felt he had betrayed the pacifist cause, for which he had striven so hard, in search of short-term physical pleasure. Muste forgave him, however, and pleaded with him to commit to a life of celibacy.

Released from solitary confinement, Bayard was intent on taking Muste's suggestion on board and unleashed his passion on the cause of desegregation, this time with a new radicalism. In May 1945, after a new set of conscientious objectors were admitted, Bayard led them in a hunger strike. Warden Haggerman now reached the end to his tether and in August 1945, he had Bayard transferred from Ashland to Lewisberg to serve the rest of term.

Lewisberg was a wholly different experience to Ashland, a tough prison with hard-timers and a no-nonsense warden who dealt with trouble makers like Bayard Rustin by separating them off from the rest of the prison population in their own dormitory. In February 1946, Bayard tried to lead a hunger strike but within two days he was being force-fed through a tube, indicating the new authoritarian approach he was up against. Perhaps realizing that continued agitation was futile, although never once compromising his principles, Bayard served the rest of his sentence with little trouble and was released in June 1946.

Passionate desegregationist
Bayard Rustin left Lewisberg with a desire to prove that the sacrifice he had made mattered. World War II had ended, but with the new era of Cold War politics beginning to crystallize, the message of pacifism was one for which society had little interest.

Race issues, however, were a different matter, as the war years had unsettled the racial status quo. Black Americans who had played their part in fighting a Nazi régime based on white supremacy, were not prepared to put up with segregation during peace time. Economic prospects had improved and it was only fair that Black America had an equal opportunity to share in this, given the collective sacrifice.

This shift in attitude was given impetus by the Supreme Court decision in Morgan v Virginia in June 1946 which rendered unconstitutional segregation on interstate transportation. As a leading member of both FOR and its civil rights offshoot CORE, Bayard Rustin threw himself into a campaign to force bus companies to adhere to the Morgan decision in what became known as the Journey of Reconciliation. This involved interracial pairs from FOR and CORE riding interstate Greyhound and Trailways buses and deliberately sitting in the segregated areas, refusing to move when bus drivers told them to as they crossed state lines. The Journey campaign saw twelve members of FOR and CORE arrested, including Bayard himself in an infamous confrontation at Chapel Hill (an arrest which was later to come back and bite him). The press attention engendered by the campaign further embedded nonviolence as part of the civil rights movement.

In September 1947, Bayard re-connected with Philip Randolph who was still interested in using Bayard's experience of nonviolence to further the civil rights cause. Bayard committed himself to Randolph's campaign to end segregation in the military. Such was Randolph's growing influence on him, that Bayard took up the campaign despite the evident contradiction between his pacifism and the aim of making it easier for black Americans to serve in the army.

From the outset the relationship between the two men was a two-way street. One can see, in Randolph's speeches during this period, his gradual adoption of the methods of nonviolence and civil disobedience in which Bayard, by this time, was so experienced. In fact, such methods became the very heart of Randolph's campaign as he called on black Americans to refuse conscription into an army which was not desegregated. Once again, Randolph's threat worked in forcing a president's hand. In 1948, President Truman issued an executive order requiring equality of treatment for all persons in the military without regard to race, colour, religion or national origin. As with his successful attempt to force Roosevelt to act six years earlier, Randolph got the credit, but one can see Bayard Rustin's influence in the more militant approach he adopted to achieve this result.

Ironically, though, the campaign resulted in a split between Bayard Rustin and Philip Randolph. The older civil rights statesman's decision to call off the campaign, in light of Truman's action, was viewed as weak by his younger protégé, who saw in the executive order ambiguities which could be used by the South to perpetuate segregation. In Bayard's view, it was Randolph rather than the President who had backed down at the crucial moment.

Bayard showed his displeasure by continuing the campaign, issuing a press release denouncing Randolph's decision. He led pickets at conscription sites calling on people to refuse to register and was arrested again, spending fourteen days in jail. Following his release, the campaign was well and truly dead, as was his relationship with Randolph; for the moment at least.

Throughout Bayard Rustin's career as a radical, however, whenever the door to a civil rights campaign closed, another would open for him to pursue his pacifist beliefs. So it proved to be, in 1948, when Bayard was sent by FOR on a five month trip to Europe and India, to further his education in Gandhian nonviolence and civil disobedience. During his time in India, Bayard met with Pandit Nehru to discuss India's non-alignment. Bayard's lectures won him many plaudits.

Back home, however, all legal avenues to overturn his arrest at Chapel Hill in the Journey for Reconciliation had been exhausted without success and Bayard was repatriated to face justice in a Southern state prison. He served twenty-two days in Roxboro, an all-black prison, during which he witnessed torture meted out to the inmates such as the brutal act of hanging them by the wrists for hours on end. Immediately on his release, he reported this barbarity, resulting in the governor overhauling disciplinary procedures and appointing a watchdog committee.

In the early 1950s, Bayard set upon a cause which fused together his commitments to peace, racial justice and nonviolence, supporting the movement for decolonization in Africa. Spending six weeks in Africa in 1952, Bayard met with Kwame Nkrumah and other African nationalists leading their countries' independence movements. This African trip energized him and on his return to the United States, he embarked on a six-week lecture tour building awareness of the independence movements in Africa, tying this to the struggle for equality in the United States. Bayard was gaining a reputation as the American Gandhi and was fast emerging as the future face of the civil rights movement.

This was all, however, about to change.

The fall and rise of Bayard Rustin
In 1953, after delivering a lecture as part of his six week tour in Pasadena, Bayard Rustin was arrested for performing lewd acts on another man in the back of a parked car. He was sentenced to sixty days in Los Angeles County Jail.

This Pasadena arrest was the turning point in Bayard Rustin's life, the moment when his trajectory to becoming a key front-line civil rights leader, ended. He would never get over it. The arrest would follow him for the rest of his life and be brought up by his enemies to highlight his homosexuality, whenever he threatened to step into the limelight. At a time when homosexuality was a crime, this incident would always come back to haunt him.

Following this conviction, Bayard fell hard. His friends abandoned him. AJ Muste in particular, who had forgiven him the first time, could not bring himself to do so again. He sacked Bayard from FOR.

On leaving jail, Bayard was faced with the daunting prospect of having to rebuild his life again. He was offered a life-line by the nascent War Resisters League which sought his organizational experience in the pacifist movement. Muste resigned from the organizational committee of the WRL when it hired Bayard, but Bayard returned its faith in him by turning it into a key organization for the anti-war movement. He wrote for its magazine, *Liberation*, going into print on his nonviolent teachings. By 1955 he seemed to have clawed himself back to the fringes of the peace movement for which he had fought so hard.

In the latter half of the 1950s, however, Bayard felt the call of the racial equality cause once more, particularly following the Supreme Court's historic ruling in *Brown v. Board of Education* in 1954. The *Brown* judgment decided that segregation was a form of inequality and hence unlawful, thereby opening the door to the prospect of revolutionary change right across society. Again it was Philip Randolph who provided Bayard Rustin with a path back into racial politics, with the formation of In Friendship, a group that provided economic aid to victims facing discrimination because they insisted on the equal status afforded to them by the *Brown* decision.

On 1 December 1955, Rosa Parkes was arrested in Montgomery Alabama for refusing to sit in the white section of the bus. The arrest precipitated a mass boycott of city buses, led by an emerging charismatic Baptist preacher named Martin Luther King, Jr. In response to the boycott, white supremacy violence erupted. King's house was bombed. Fearing that the black community would meet violence with violence, precipitating a race war, Randolph again proved instrumental in the career of Bayard Rustin.

He decided that Bayard's presence in Montgomery was necessary to put the theory of nonviolent resistance into full practice.

With Randolph's backing, Bayard was immediately exposed to the leaders of the boycott, including both King and Ralph Abernathy. Bayard's impact was immediate. He drafted speeches for them on the theme of nonviolence. He came up with the idea that those indicted for the boycott should present themselves to the court house dressed in their finest clothes, holding themselves out as proud of what they had done, rather than waiting at home to be arrested like criminals. The move had a massive positive impact on the mood of the black community and left white community leaders flabbergasted.

Bayard established himself as a key adviser to King and mentored him on the theory of nonviolence. In so doing, Bayard transformed King into one of the greatest proponents of nonviolence the world has ever seen. This in itself made Bayard Rustin a key driving force behind what was to become the most powerful social movement of the twentieth century.

At around this time, Bayard wrote an article in *Liberation* in King's name, drawing together the strands of racial inequality and economic inequality and marrying them up with the new and powerful force of nonviolent resistance. It was also Bayard who put King directly in touch with Randolph, a relationship mediated by Bayard, and which was to become vital to the civil rights movement in the following years.

From the articles he produced in this period, one can see Bayard positioning the civil rights movement in a broader historical context which gave it increasing power. He saw the Montgomery boycott as akin to the opening salvos in the American Revolution and equated the struggle for racial equality with the nation utilizing its newfound industrial might for the benefit of all and not just the white elite, thereby building the Founding Fathers' goal of an ever more perfect union. However, he was also strongly of the view that organization was needed to build the Montgomery boycotts into a mass movement across the South. The result was a two-day meeting in Atlanta which brought together sixty leaders from twenty-nine different communities, calling on blacks to resist segregation with nonviolent resistance. The organization would eventually form into the Southern Christian Leadership Conference, one of the principle organizations of the civil rights movement. Throughout the rest of the 1950s, Bayard applied himself to ensuring that its leader, Martin Luther King, Jr. would become the movement's national leader.

In 1957, Bayard worked frenetically for King's "Crusade for Citizenship" to push for voter registration of blacks in the South, following the passage of legislation to investigate voting rights violations. The Crusade, however, had little success principally because, although Bayard outlined the plan for it, his Pasadena conviction prevented him from being part of its implementation. The dynamic of frenetic action, followed by retreat from the limelight to avoid embarrassing the cause, was to be one continually repeated during the rest of Bayard Rustin's career. His absence, however, would always demonstrate all the more the value of his organizational skills, something that King desperately lacked.

The outset of the 1960s saw the civil rights movement galvanized with a slew of sit-ins at colleges across the South as students challenged segregation at lunch counters. At around this time Martin Luther King, Jr. was indicted for tax evasion. Bayard jumped into the fray, by organizing the King Defense Committee and raising a mass petition in support. He saw this as the opportunity to push King and the SCLC further into the national consciousness, dislodging the more conservative NAACP as the leading civil rights organization. The NAACP had always been lukewarm on the tactic of nonviolence and this, Bayard thought, would always hold the movement back. Indeed,

Bayard hoped the newfound momentum he was galvanizing for King would come together in a project he was organizing, to picket both the Republican and Democratic Party conventions in election year.

Again, however, Bayard fell foul of his past. Adam Powell, a rival to King, threatened to spread unfounded rumours of an affair between King and Bayard. Despite there being no truth to the rumours, the threat was enough to concern King. In response, Bayard resigned from formally assisting the SCLC. The 1960 convention demonstrations went ahead, but again without Bayard's organizational flair, their impact was muted. The incident was a reminder of Bayard Rustin's brilliance, but also the limitations he had to work within because he was homosexual. He had the ability to be so much more than just an invisible force behind many of the key civil rights projects. Because of who he was, however -- a homosexual in a world where it was illegal to be so -- Bayard knew he had to step away, so as not to risk the cause for which he strove.

Once again, it was Philip Randolph who brought Bayard out of the cold. Randolph hated how Bayard would always be cut down by his past, just when he was on the verge of coming to prominence. He asked Bayard to come and work for him, but Bayard this time politely declined. Instead, he returned to the peace movement and travelled to India to attend the War Resisters International triennial conference, before travelling on to the United Kingdom where he worked with the Campaign for Nuclear Disarmament to organize a peace walk across Europe. He then helped organize an international peace brigade, going with it on a mission to Africa to promote the ongoing freedom struggles in the continent.

In his absence, the civil rights movement continued to gain momentum in the United States, principally in the face of the obduracy of the Kennedy administration, which did little to act on behalf of racial justice, for fear of rocking the boat with key constituent members of the Democratic Party. Bayard kept some connection with the civil rights movement during 1961 and 1962, in particular by participating in debates with Malcolm X, arguing against the black separatist militancy which this new charismatic leader was proposing. But Bayard felt like an observer, rather than a participant, as the movement slowly built to a crescendo. All that, however, was about to change.

Architect of the civil rights movement's greatest day
Of all the civil rights and peace movement leaders whom Bayard had worked for during his long career as a dissident, only one had stood by him through thick and thin: A. Philip Randolph. It had been Randolph whose influence had first brought Bayard into the civil rights movement, tapping his experience of nonviolence to fight for desegregation in the military, following his release from Lewisberg. It had been Randolph who had forgiven Bayard for his open criticism, after Randolph had called off this campaign. It had been Randolph, who had brought Bayard back into the movement after his Pasedena arrest, through the creation of In Friendship. It had been Randolph who had sent Bayard to Montgomery, where he had taught Martin Luther King, Jr. the theory of nonviolence.

Now it was Bayard's to turn to repay the unbending support which Randolph, a man twenty years his senior, had always given him in what must be one of the most famous acts of reverse mentoring in history.

Randolph, the doyen of the civil rights movement, had first shot to national notoriety in 1942 when his threatened march on Washington had forced the hand of President Roosevelt to desegregate the defence industries. Having elicited Roosevelt's concession in 1942, Randolph had called off the march. In the same way he had called off the anti-conscription campaign when he had forced President Truman to desegregate the armed forces five years later. By 1963, however, Randolph still felt there was something missing from the civil rights movement. He believed the search for racial equality needed to be married up with the issue of economic justice, for it to reach its full potential. In this respect, he and Bayard Rustin were of the same mind.

In December 1962, Bayard paid a visit to Randolph's home. They talked expansively of how black injustice was tied to a society that kept them economically dependent and poor. They reminisced about past campaigns, both won and lost, about Randolph's 1942 threatened march, about Rustin's experience of civil disobedience through nonviolence. Suddenly, all their collective experience thoughts and memories seemed to coalesce. Neither could remember who first mentioned the idea, but when the evening was done, the potent mix of the older man's experience of standing up to Presidents and the younger man's continued passion for agitation led to the proposal that was to change American society forever: The March on Washington for Jobs and Freedom.[33]

When the two men took soundings from others in the movement, they were met with nothing but enthusiasm. Indeed, the Birmingham Alabama protests in 1962, driven by Martin Luther King. Jr, provided momentum for national action. In Alabama 500 students had been arrested, and images of snarling police dogs biting at the legs of teenagers, under the brutal leadership of Police Chief Bull Connor, were broadcast across the nation's television screens.

The Big Six civil rights organizations were now convinced by Philip Randolph and Bayard Rustin's idea for nationwide action. Bayard himself had drawn up the organizational framework for the March which would see the process put in the hands of a single director under the supervision of a committee on which each of the Big Six were to be represented. Every one of them knew that Bayard was the one person with the organizational experience to pull the whole thing off. Again, however, at the crucial moment it seemed that Bayard's past would intervene to present the civil rights movement form utilising his talent to the full.

On 2 July 1963 the Big Six civil rights leaders came together to make key decisions on the March. Roy Wilkins of the NAACP cleared the room, so that it was only the six of them present. He told the others that he could not support Bayard Rustin as director. Bayard had too many scars: his association with communism in the 1940s but principally, his Pasadena arrest. Four of the other leaders either agreed, or like King, were careful not to take sides.

The sixth was Randolph and in a monumental show of support for his young mentor, he came up with a solution that outmaneuvered his peers. Randolph told them that he himself would assume the nominal role of director. But he must have the freedom to appoint his own deputy, to whom he would delegate the organizational details. He told them that he wanted Bayard Rustin as his deputy.[34] None of the other five could say no to this, not to a man of Philip Randolph's standing. And so America had its day.

In the ensuing eight weeks, Rustin worked night and day to organize the event. It must have felt that the totality of his life's experience had been building up to make this moment happen. He galvanized the Big Six organisations to get their membership out. He went on the radio to broadcast the need to march. He led training sessions in nonviolence for hundreds of volunteers.

The authorities did their best to dampen the effect of the mass call for action, making it known that there would be a large police presence. J. Edgar Hoover's FBI was in overdrive releasing information to damage reputations, and in Bayard Rustin they had an easy target. First his early associations with communism were publicly revealed, leading to calls for him to step down as the organizer. Randolph refused, calling Rustin, "Mr March-on-Washington".[35] Then Storm Thurmond, the Senator from South Carolina who had broken from the Democratic Party to run for president in 1948, stepped into the fray to launch an all-out attack on Bayard Rustin in the Senate. Fed by information provided by Hoover, Thurmond put the Pasedena incident and Bayard's entire arrest sheet into the Congressional Record, making Bayard Rustin at that moment the most famous homosexual in America.

Randolph's response to Thurmond's attack was unequivocal. On behalf of the entire black leadership, Randolph voiced complete confidence in Bayard Rustin's character. He went on to state, "I am dismayed that there are in this country men who, wrapping themselves in the mantle of Christian morality, would mutilate the most elementary conceptions of human decency, privacy and humility in order to persecute other men."[36] With those words, Randolph killed any further probing questions on Bayard Rustin's sexuality.

So it came to be that on 23 August 1963, two-hundred and fifty thousand people gathered at the Washington Memorial. Following a prelude of song, the speeches began. Slowly they built to a crescendo, and what a crescendo it was. Martin Luther King, Jr. took to the stage and America had its, "I have a dream" moment.

The 1963 March will forever be associated with King's speech and it is often forgotten what happened after the roar of the crowd had died down. It was at this moment that Bayard Rustin took to the stage to introduce Philip Randolph. Randolph enumerated the demands of the March and Bayard finished by leading the crowd in a recitation of a pledge to continue the struggle. It was a fitting end to America's greatest day, a day which had come about because of the intertwining of these two men's lives in a mentoring relationship that changed the world.

The power of reverse mentoring to promote change

In the relationship between Philip Randolph and Bayard Rustin we see the true power of reverse mentorship. We also learn from the relationship several of the key traits necessary to make reverse mentoring work.

Randolph was in his fifties when he first met Rustin. Having forced Roosevelt to change the law in 1942, he had already become one of the most respected figures in the civil rights movement. Randolph was, in short, at the very height of his powers, influence and experience. Yet he seems to have realized, whether consciously or not, that in achieving his elevated status, he had also reached the outer limits of his experience. To move forward, Randolph appreciated he needed to break free from the limits his own experience had imposed. He needed to be open to learning new things from younger members of the civil rights movement and in Bayard Rustin (then in his late twenties) he saw the perfect person to teach him.

At a young age, Bayard Rustin had already steeped himself in the teachings of Gandhi to further his pacifist beliefs. He had learned the disciplined practice of nonviolent resistance and civil disobedience. He had been beaten in prison, but had destroyed the spirit of his attacker by sitting there and taking it, pushing the warden into making concessions on desegregation as a result. He had boldly stood firm and constantly agitated as a conscientious objector. It was this new nonviolent militancy which Randolph wanted to tap in order to take the civil rights movement in a new direction and he opened his mind to learning more from a man twenty years his junior.

This then is the first valuable trait we learn: the need by the older protégé to recognize the limits of his or her own experience and have an appreciation that breaking free from those limits requires an openness to new and younger ideas.

Secondly, we learn of the unbending trust and support needed to underpin a relationship of reverse mentorship. Bayard Rustin was a homosexual man in a society which made it illegal to be one. Prejudice against homosexuals was not just an ingrained societal trait, it was underpinned by the force of law. Following his Pasadena arrest, Bayard spent the rest of his life learning who his real friends were.

His first mentor, AJ Muste of FOR abandoned him. Although Bayard mentored Martin Luther King, Jr. in civil disobedience, King would repeatedly distance himself from Bayard whenever his past threatened to make him a liability. Only Randolph unquestioningly stood by Bayard Rustin. Even when Bayard attacked him in the press release in 1948 for calling off his campaign against the Truman administration, Randolph seems to have been forgiving. At so many crucial points in Rustin's life when there seemed no way back, Randolph showed him the path.

Only this level of trust and ability to forgive can produce the openness required to achieve the true potential of reverse mentoring. This extraordinary potential is the third thing we learn from these two men. That December evening in 1962, when the two men got together, they talked as equals with no issues off-limits in their conversation and no idea too crazy to be voiced, such was the level of trust and openness between them. It is somehow fitting that neither can remember who first came up with the idea for the march on Washington, for we see in this how it emerged from their partnership being greater than the sum of its parts. That evening, the experience of Philip Randolph had its limits removed by the skill, boldness and intelligence of Bayard Rustin.

Randolph put his newly unfettered experience to forceful use in that moment when the Big Six civil rights leaders met to choose the director who would organize the March. Having been told it could not be Bayard Rustin by Roy Wilkins of the powerful NAACP, we see Randolph combining his experience with some nonviolent negotiation jujitsu he may well have picked up from the influence of his younger mentor. Taking Wilkins attack on the chin, Randolph offered himself up as the director to organize the March, and then utilized his considerable experience as a defence. Could Wilkins really say "no" to the appointment of the man who had made Roosevelt and Truman back down? Of course not. Nor could he deny Randolph freedom of choice on his deputy director. The path was clear for Bayard Rustin to step into the limelight.

An openness to learning, complete trust and forgiveness and a combination which makes the sum of its parts so much greater than the whole: these are the three traits which Philip Randolph and Bayard Rustin teach us are needed to enable a reverse mentoring relationship to reach its full potential. Most of all, however, these two men stand as examples to the extraordinary results which can be achieved when that full potential is reached. In utilizing reverse mentorship, we not only aim to capture that potential for ourselves, we also embrace the legacy of two men who successfully used the dynamic to change humanity for the better.

Chapter 8

THE STEPPING-STONE TO GENIUS

It takes years to build expertise and hone one's skill-set. It requires dedication, hard graft, practice, trial-and-error and sheer bloody-mindedness to stick with it. Those prepared to put in the hours will eventually reach the pinnacle, the moment when they are acknowledged as reaching the top of their profession, when they are branded with the label of "expert".

Yet the further onward leap from expert to genius is elusive to most. This takes something more than just will-power and an ability to grind it out. Genius requires an opening up of the mind. It requires a playfulness of thought, a desire to expose one's expertise to new and completely unrelated areas of knowledge, because when connections are drawn between two entirely unconnected ideas, that's when the magic happens. That's when quantum leaps in logic take place, boundaries are extended and genius is reached.

Opening one's mind like this is hard, however, particularly for the expert. Expertise is created through years of conditioning one's thought process into a disciplined structure and away from the ability to make tangential steps which would have occurred to no one else. The leap from expert to genius effectively involves the embracing of a contradiction. It requires the expert to become counter-intuitive, to go against everything his instinct is telling him and make connections no one else would think about. This is why genius is so limited and achieved by so few. This is why we are led to believe that genius is unattainable except by the few who are already born with it, that it is something congenitally ingrained in one's DNA right from the outset. Genius is nature, not nurture, we are told. It is not something that can be learned.

Yet history is sprinkled with examples that suggest otherwise and demonstrate that the leap to genius is open to the most ordinary of us. All we need is the right outside influence or indeed the right mentor to provide the spark to blow away the limitations that fetter our expertise and set our minds free.

Winston Churchill's path to power

Winston Churchill stands on the shoulders of titans as one of the greatest figures of the twentieth century, if not of all history. His leadership of Britain during the Second World War made him the saviour of his nation and indeed of the civilization many of us enjoy today, a civilization based on democratic government, freedom and individual rights.

Turn back the clock to May 1940 for a moment, a time when all seemed lost for a forlorn and pitiful Britain. Hitler had run roughshod across Europe. Fascist dictatorships governed in Germany, Italy and Spain. Russia had signed the Nazi-Soviet pact and the two despotic regimes had carved up Poland like a Sunday roast chicken. Panzer divisions had swept through Belgium and French resistance had melted faster than butter in the summer sun. Objectively considered, by this point Hitler had won the war. The entire continent and its resources were under his control. There was no prospect of the United States coming to the rescue, either. At that time, it would have been politically impossible for Franklin Delano Roosevelt to end his country's isolationism, and propping up the British Empire was something to which the President was vehemently ideologically opposed.

Britain stood on its own, completely exposed and poised for invasion. The country was like an unarmed ten-pound weakling in the shadow of an irate bully carrying a baseball bat, itching to vent his nihilistic Nietzschean anger. The British government's complete failure to heed

Churchill's warnings of German militarism build-up during the 1930s, had left it completely unprepared to defend the nation and the civilization for which it stood. Only the thin sliver of the English Channel stood between Britain and the Nazi juggernaut. "Operation Sea Lion", Hitler's planned invasion of Britain, was within touching distance of being ready for launch.

This was the situation facing the British nation, when the post of Prime Minister was offered to Winston Churchill. How easy would it have been for him to have said, "You've got to be kidding me!" How tempting must it have been to reply: "I've been telling you this would happen for years, but did you listen? No. And now you expect me to fix this mess? Come on!"

This perhaps would have been the normal human reaction. Especially given what Churchill had been through. For a decade, he had been cast aside as the ultimate political failure, a living, breathing example of wasted talent, a lesson in hubristic over-reaching. Parliament viewed him as an annoying anachronism. His warnings about war were treated as the ramblings of an old man, a war-monger from yesteryear. He was like that annoying long-winded Uncle you get stuck talking to at Christmas dinner, someone you tolerate because you have to, not because he has anything worth saying. In 1940, Churchill was sixty-five years old, the age at which most of us retire. Who could have blamed him, if he had walked away saying, "I told you so"?

But walking away from a challenge was not in Churchill's DNA. Especially a challenge which threatened to destroy everything for which he and Britain stood. This was the moment his entire life had been building up to. In his mind, fate had put him on this earth for this challenge.

And what a mind he had! It was a mind conditioned by self-teaching and willpower. Churchill's schooling had left him seemingly at the lower end of any formal academic scale. He did not do well in examinations. He would gladly have displayed his vast knowledge of poetry, history and military battles, this last developed through playing with his toy soldiers as a child. Sadly, all these examinations served to do was expose his ignorance of Latin and mathematics – subjects in which he had little interest.[37] Instead, it was up to Churchill to absorb the things that his formal education had not provided. He achieved this whilst doing a stint with the 4th Hussars in Bangalore in India. Policing the Empire was a lackadaisical affair, leaving much free time, on those unbearably hot afternoons, for the young Churchill to absorb the writings of Gibbon and Macaulay, Plato and Aristotle, Malthus and Darwin.[38]

Coupled with reading, he catapulted himself into the world's hotspots as a journalist to gather experience. Whilst his peers were learning at university, Churchill was sucking the marrow out of the university of life, pulling every string he could to be part of the Spanish forces fighting a guerilla war in Cuba, accompanying the Malakand Field Force to Afghanistan and partaking in the British army's last cavalry charge at Omdurman. Then came his infamous involvement in the Boer War, where as a young correspondent he was taken captive after the armoured train he was on was ambushed. He was made a prisoner of war at Pretoria, embarked on a daring escape and became the Boer's most wanted man, with a price of twenty-five pounds sterling on his head, dead or alive. His successful escape thrust him into the public limelight and Churchill fully capitalized on this with his first excursion into politics, becoming Member of Parliament for Oldham. He was twenty-six years old and had by this tender age gathered more experience than normal human beings squeeze into three life-times.

Government posts quickly followed. As under-secretary for the colonies in 1903 he oversaw the grant of self-government to the Transvaal and the Orange Free State and the union of South Africa. At thirty-three years old he was made President of the Board of Trade, his first cabinet position, where he teamed up with Lloyd George, the

Chancellor of the Exchequer, to lend support to the famous budget of 1909 which introduced unemployment insurance and non-contributory pensions and led to reform of the House of Lords in 1910. He then became Home Secretary, one of the three big offices of state, where he made himself unpopular with the unions. After this, in 1911, it was on to the Admiralty, a position he loved and threw himself into with all the energy he could muster, bringing in reforms which improved conditions for working-level sailors and, most importantly, making Britain's navy war ready.

In 1914 Germany invaded Belgium, marking the onset of the First World War, and quickly the outdated strategies of both sides created the horrific stalemate of trench warfare on the Western Front, where a generation of young men was lost, hurled into the path of machine-gun fire with futile repeated charges into no-man's land to gain yards of wasteland. Churchill pushed for a new strategy to break this despicable deadlock. It involved hitting the enemy in its soft underbelly in Southern Europe, knocking Turkey out of the war and opening up an eastern front to put pressure on the German lines. But the Dardanelles campaign, the manifestation of this strategy, turned out to be an unmitigated disaster, resulting in the loss of 180,000 lives, most of them on the failed landings on the beach at Gallipoli. In May 1915, Churchill was forced to resign from office in humiliation.

In an astonishing act of penance, one never previously embarked upon by any politician forced to resign in failure before or since, Churchill left Britain to serve as a lieutenant colonel in the very same trenches on the Western Front, which the Dardanelles campaign had failed to relieve. For Churchill, it was a chastening experience, but one he threw himself into with characteristic energy, improving the morale of the men serving under him.

In 1917, Lloyd George brought Churchill back in from the cold as Minister of Munitions, after which he was shunted round to the position of Colonial Secretary, in which he served until 1922, when the coalition government fell. Churchill lost his Parliamentary seat in the ensuing election. After two years spent writing his history of the First World War, he was back in Parliament again and, in an astonishing revival of fortunes, he was appointed by Prime Minister Stanley Baldwin as Chancellor of the Exchequer, a position he occupied until 1929.

Then came the Wilderness Years of the 1930s, the decade in which Churchill – as a backbench Member of Parliament – was passed over for governmental office by successive Prime Ministers. This was the decade when Churchill looked on in horror at the rise of Hitler and the resurgence of German nationalism. He was the only politician of any standing who saw Hitler's actions as a threat to peace in Europe. He threw himself into writing articles and speaking publicly to try to force the government to see what he saw.

Germany left the League of Nations in 1933, seized the Rhineland in 1935 and the Sudeten Lands in Czechoslovakia in 1938. On each occasion, Churchill's warnings about a coming conflict were ignored and even dismissed as the reactionary ramblings of a war-monger well past his prime. Peace in our time was what the British public wanted. A piece of paper signed by Hitler, making that promise, was what Neville Chamberlain gave them on his return from Munich in 1938.

Munich proved to be exactly the mistake Churchill had foretold. Hitler must have signed the treaty with his fingers crossed behind his back. No sooner was the ink dry, than his Panzers were steaming across the border into Poland, their tire tracks marking the beginning of World War II.

When words are the only weapons

So it is that in September 1939, Britain finds herself at war with Germany, isolated and completely unprepared. Onwards proceeds the Nazi advance through Belgium, into France. Soon French capitulation leaves everything in

Western Europe under Hitler's control. Everything that is, except Britain, but it seems only a matter of time.

Then, at that moment when the German army reaches French shores, when its guns turn north towards the unprotected British Isles and plans for invasion are being finalized, that is when the country calls for Winston Churchill, the one man who predicted this would happen all along. Astonishingly too, for whatever reason, Hitler chooses this precise moment, via back-channel negotiations, to offer a peace settlement.

Key members of Churchill's new cabinet gather together. The main voices are in favour of accepting it. Looked at in terms of pure numbers, this would seem the entirely logical thing to do. A simple comparison of German military might with British military weakness, with the former poised to hurl itself at the latter, would have led anyone to the inexorable conclusion that defeat and failure are inevitable. So why not, in the circumstances, go for a deal?

But in defiance of all this logic, Churchill says "no".

Revisionist historians have criticized him for this, but Churchill was right. Hitler had never complied with any agreement with any country and there was nothing to suggest that he would have complied with any peace terms with the British longer than was convenient to him.[39] So, in the summer of 1940, Britain is at war and poised for Hitler's invasion with a fig leaf of outdated arms to defend herself with.

Faced with this situation, Churchill did something which changed the course of history. Through his boundless energy, meeting with people up and down the country and most of all, through a series of some of the most sublime speeches the world has ever known, he convinced the British people to stand firm and believe they were somehow, some day, going to win this thing.

With these speeches, Churchill proved the power of oratory to lift people's souls to lofty heights. He made people believe that they were fighting for a cause, so much larger than themselves, that they were the defenders of a civilization built on freedoms handed down from previous generations to the men and women of this age to defend. Now those freedoms were in the gravest of perils and the nation had to stand firm and fight. He imbued the country with a sense of mission and belief that no matter what things looked like now, they could and would find a path to ultimate victory.

In short, Churchill made an entire nation defy the logic of the horrible circumstances stacked against it. He pulled together a country to work as a collective unit towards the singular aim of victory no matter what the cost. In doing so, Winston Churchill touched the face of greatness and changed the course of history.

Pure genius: these are the only words which truly capture Churchill's ability as speech maker during those summer months of 1940 when invasion was imminent and all seemed lost. As Kennedy said twenty years later of Churchill, "He marshalled the English language and sent it into battle".[40] So true, but lest we forget, with little in the way of munitions, words were the only weapons Churchill had.

The phrases from his sublime, epoch-defining oratory of this period packed a punch that put the Panzers to shame. Churchill's adjective-filled, repetitive, somewhat archaic language, spoken in his familiar rumbling tones, have become immortal. We start three days after his appointment as Prime Minister, when on 13 May 1940, Churchill addressed the House of Commons with his "blood, toil, tears and sweat" speech, laying out his policy of "victory, victory at all costs, victory in spite of all terror, victory, however long and hard the road may be; for without victory, there is no survival".[41]

Then on 4 June 1940, the last day of the Dunkirk evacuation, Churchill stirred the nation with these unforgettable lines: "we shall fight on the beaches, we shall fight on the landing grounds, we shall fight in the fields and in the streets, we shall fight in the hills; we shall never surrender."[42]

On 18 June 1940, addressing the nation to explain the capitulation of France and to galvanize morale for the Battle of Britain that was about to begin, Churchill called on every man and woman to brace themselves for their duties, "and so bear ourselves that, if the British Empire and its Commonwealth last for a thousand years, men will still say, 'This was their finest hour.'"[43]

Churchill's oratory drew on every essence of experience he had gathered. His speeches were not off the cuff, but masterpieces into which every ounce of energy, thought and preparation were poured. Every word was weighed for its impact, every phrase tested for its power. We are taught today to speak from power-points and make it all sound conversational, but this run-of-the mill "presentations skills" style would have been anathema to Churchill. From the very first speech he made, he knew the power of scripting, rehearsal, memorization and practice, rolling every adjective round his tongue several times to find the right pitch, nuance and impact. Conversational presentation is everyday, mundane and soon forgotten. True oratory is for the special occasion and provides a performance which lives forever.

Winston Churchill always demanded the complete performance of himself, one riven with heart and soul. He was an actor with lines he had himself written and memorized, one who was playing the part of a warrior from ancient Greece, steeped in the art of oratory, lifting the spirits of his nation. This was the man who had taught himself Macaulay's *Lays of Ancient Rome* and devoured Gibbon's *Decline and Fall of the Roman Empire*. The language he used was not the type used in everyday conversation and it was not supposed to be. It was language handed down from the past and mobilized brilliantly for present use, by a practitioner whose years of experience made him an expert in what he did.

Winnie and "The Few"

But even experts need help now and then. Even experts at inspiring themselves need inspiration from somewhere. And for perhaps one of his most memorable speeches, Churchill benefited from the dynamic of reverse mentoring to find that inspiration. The young men fighting the war would lead him to discover a set of words which would bring Churchill to the pinnacle of oratorical artistry and imbue a nation which such pride and emotion, as to change the British character forever.

The month is August 1940. Churchill is visiting Fighter Command's 11 Group Operations Room bunker in Uxbridge, at a moment when the Battle of Britain is raging. Hitler is aiming to break British will-power by attempting to bomb her cities into oblivion and gain control of the skies. It is from this bunker in Uxbridge that the defence of the primary battle ground – the skies over London and south east England – is being marshalled.

Churchill sits on a balcony, as beneath him the air controllers guide pilots of Spitfires and Hurricanes to intercept and engage incoming bombers and their Luftwaffe escorts. Counters are moved round a huge map like chess pieces on a board, keeping track of the approaching enemy. Churchill watches spellbound as squadron after squadron is committed to the air, not knowing whether it will return.

At one point Churchill asks Air Vice-Marshall Sir Keith Park what other reserves are available, when all squadrons are airborne. Park replies that there are none. This is how the war is being fought, with nothing being held back and everything being thrown into the fray. At one point tears stream down Churchill's face.

Before he leaves the bunker that day for the sixteen-mile journey back to Chequers, Churchill makes a point of congratulating everyone personally for their immense effort. He is full of emotion as he gets into his car with General Hastings Lionel "Pug" Ismay.

"Don't speak to me," Churchill says to Pug as they drive away, "I have never been so moved."

For months now, Churchill must have been under the greatest unrelenting mental stress of any Prime Minister past or present. He has chaired well over one hundred cabinet meetings, listened as his advisers argue points before him, and made countless of life and death decisions, often imposing his will when all around him disagree. His black dispatch bag is never less than full to bursting with memos. It has been a massive pressure to live with, day in, day out.

Now in the back of that car, the mix of stress and emotion at seeing the Battle of Britain waged with everything the RAF (the Royal Air Force) has, overwhelms Churchill. A five-minute silence ensues as he sits there, lost in his thoughts about what he has just witnessed.

He thinks about how each counter moved around that board back at Uxbridge represents the life of a pilot from the RAF, being thrown into battle at a moment's notice. The average age of the pilots fighting this war is twenty. Some are even as young as eighteen, not old enough to vote, but old enough to fight in the life and death struggle their country is locked in with the Nazis. On the shoulders of these brave few young men, rests the fate of civilization.

It is this realization that pounds Churchill with the juggernaut of pride and emotion throbbing through his chest in those five minutes of silence. A cocktail of inspiration takes form and – powered on by the months of stress and the youthful bravery he has witnessed – that powerful mind goes to work in formulating the right mix of words to be worthy of this moment.

When Churchill breaks his silence, it is with an oratorical masterpiece: "Never in the field of human conflict has so much been owed by so many to so few."[44]

Days later, Churchill utters this sentence in his speech to Parliament and in so doing makes the nation feel as proud and emotional as he did in that five minute spell of genius on the ride back to Chequers. It is a moment inspired entirely by the young pilots who would decide the fate of the war. And from the moment those words are uttered in the House, "The Few" is how the RAF fighter pilots become known. With that, Churchill imbues the public with an immense sense of gratitude and pride in the enormity of what these pilots are doing for their country and he lifts the spirit of the nation to demonstrate the same level of bravery for the rest of the war.

Formulating a nation's character
The power of Churchill's speeches during the months of May to September 1940 cannot be underestimated. His words and indeed his whole persona had an impact on many of his compatriots, convincing them of the role they had to play in the greatest drama their nation had ever faced. The Blitz never broke the British people's morale. They learned to live with the terrifying nightly bombing raids as an inconvenience. This "stiff upper lip" characteristic, the ability to "keep buggering on" – another of Churchill's immortal phrases – in the face of all inconvenience and hardship, has become a particular British character trait because of Churchill. We see it still in the way commuters put up with trains being late, or being stuck on the Tube in between tunnels, with nothing but self-deprecating humour to keep them going through the boredom. This is what it means to be British. This is the British character Churchill gave us.

As for "The Few", who so inspired Churchill, they have rightly taken their place in the pantheon of greatness for what they achieved. Historians record 15 September 1940 as the date on which the Battle of Britain was won. This was the day that Goering launched his massive raid to try to break the RAF once and for all. But the Few stood firm and fought the Luftwaffe to a standstill, which was victory enough. The previous day, Hitler had announced that his plans for his sea invasion of Britain were complete. All he needed was enough air cover to give the go-ahead. The RAF, however, denied him that and the invasion had to be postponed. Instead, Hitler turned his attention east to Russia, breaking his pact with Stalin as he had broken every other agreement he had entered into. The opening of the second front in the east provided a massive turning point in the war and the first stepping-stone on the path to victory in which Churchill made his country believe.

As for Winton Churchill himself, he has gone down in history as the greatest Briton of all time, saving his country from invasion and the world from tyranny. A lesser known achievement is that in 1953 Churchill was awarded the Nobel Prize for Literature. This award has been masked somewhat by the other massive successes of his extraordinary life. But it was an award which Churchill himself delighted in, one which recognized his genius with words, the mastery of which enabled him to save a civilization.

But lest we forget, on that day at the bunker in Uxbridge, it took the actions of youth to fire Churchill's emotion, and inspire the phraseology that lifted a nation as one, in complete gratitude to The Few who had saved it. In Churchill's words, the power of youth and experience blended together and created something so much greater than the sum of its parts, in a testament to the dynamic power of reverse mentoring.

Chapter 9

ACHIEVING TRUE PURPOSE THROUGH
REVERSE MENTORING

We are told we should all have a purpose in life, a path we should follow in order to fulfill the set of values by which we live. This is easy to say, but finding one's purpose is difficult to achieve. There is no shop from which a purpose can be bought, no obvious platform from which they are distributed to us in nice downloadable forms at the start of our lives. No, a purpose is something we have to discover for ourselves and constantly re-affirm, often through a process of struggle, self-discovery and inquiry.

If we think hard enough, we can all identify someone we know who understands their true purpose in life. It may not be obvious at first because purpose-driven people do not shout it from the roof tops. They do, however, possess certain characteristics which make them stand out. A quiet confidence that comes from knowing what they have to do to the exclusion of every other distraction. A tranquility that gives them a sense of balance and an ability never to lose their cool. They are deeply caring without letting their passions overrun. They listen when others speak, because they are constantly searching for opportunities to exert their values. They speak only when they have something to say. They are entirely self-effacing and never blow their own trumpet because they are confident in their own path and recognize ego as the ultimate energy-sapping and pointless distraction it is.

Ultimately, we should all be challenged to find our true purpose. Each one of us should ask ourselves, "Why do I do what I do?" and we should struggle with this question until the answer emerges. It is only through this kind of struggle that our purpose is carved into our character and becomes part of us.

To assist us in finding an answer, however, we need the right tools. One of the best tools at our disposal in this journey of self-discovery, is reverse mentoring.

Understanding purpose

To understand why reverse mentoring provides the perfect pathway to purpose, the work of the American psychologist Abraham Maslow is relevant.

Maslow formulated a theory called the "hierarchy of needs" to explain why we as human beings do what we do.[45] According to Maslow, every human being has five ascending levels of need which we are driven to try to satisfy throughout our lives.

The first level is the need to satisfy our basic physical requirements, such as obtaining the food and water we need to survive. Once these basic physical needs are met, we move to the second level: the need for safety. Hence, we contribute to a pension scheme or purchase insurance to ensure we are kept safe in the future and in times of trouble. The third level is the need for love and belonging, hence we form relationships and start families. The fourth level is the need for self-esteem, to feel accepted and valued by others, which drives our choice of career or the hobbies in which we participate.

These first four levels of need, Maslow classes as "deficit needs", such that if the particular need is not met, it creates a deficit or gap which the person is naturally motivated to replenish or fill. Once the need is met and the deficit is replenished, however, it ceases to motivate. Deficit needs, in other words, motivate through the craving their absence stimulates, rather like being cold motivates one to find warmth. Once the need has been satisfied, the craving ends.

It is in Maslow's fifth level of need, however, that we find the concept of purpose. This is the need for self-actualization. Maslow never offered a full definition of self-actualization, but it can be summarized as this: finding and then living by one's true purpose.

For example, unlike the first four "deficit" needs, self-actualization is classed by Maslow as a "being need". Whereas a "deficit need" motivates by means of the craving which the deficit creates until it is satisfied, a "being need" motivates by the continued achievement of the need. In other words, whilst a "deficit" need ceases once the need has been met, achieving a "being need" stimulates the desire to keep fulfilling it. It is, in this sense, a growth motivation. The more one accomplishes through self-actualization, the more one grows and deepens as a human being and the more one wants to continue along this pathway.

Self-actualization, then, is akin to finding one's purpose and then directing one's entire life towards fulfillment, or actualization of that purpose. Indeed, through biographical analysis, that is through studying historical figures who fell within the category of self-actualizers (such as Abraham Lincoln, Albert Einstein, Jane Addams, Eleanor Roosevelt and Baruch Spinoza) Maslow identified a collection of character traits that define a person who has achieved self-actualization. These included:
* An ability to see what is genuine from what is fake and dishonest;
* An approach to life's difficulties which sees them as problems to be solved and overcome, rather than grievances to be complained about or succumbed to in victimhood.
* A recognition that life is not necessarily about finding a means to a given end or destination, but realizing that it is often the means or the journey itself, and how it is conducted, that counts.
* A liking for solitude and inner contemplation, coupled with an approach to relationships that leads to fewer, but much deeper friendships than other people have.

* The possession of an autonomous and independent mind that resists pressure to conform and fit in, if that goes against one's core values
* The possession of a sense of humour that is not hostile to others but self-deprecating
* The instinct to accept others for who they are, coupled with a sense of compassion for humanity that is underpinned by a strong sense of ethics and which manifests itself in a personality of humility and respect.
* The ability to be spontaneous with an almost child-like simplicity which continuously sees the world with wonder.
* The ability to be inventive and creative.
* Through the achievement of "peak experiences", an ability to transcend and appreciate they are part of something much bigger and infinite than the finite limitation which their lives provide.

These, then, are the characteristics of self-actualization. These are character traits of someone who knows their purpose in life and is attuned to the core values by which they must live.

So where does reverse mentoring come in?

The answer lies in the leap that needs to be made to get from Maslow's fourth level of need – that of self-esteem – to the highest level he identifies: self-actualization. As indicated, self-esteem is a deficit need, one that we crave to satisfy through our career choice, club-memberships and the accumulation of outward recognition. We see in the human craving for self-esteem, the bias that society has created in favour of experience. Indeed, the gathering of experience in the form of line-items we put on our Curriculum Vitae is precisely how the search for self-esteem manifests itself and why there is such a great emphasis placed on this.

However, the step from self-esteem to self-actualization is, according to Maslow, very rarely achieved. Perhaps the reason for this lies in the constraints of experience, which Maslow's need for self-esteem brings into sharp focus. Self-esteem, which is built by experience, is a craving that needs to be satisfied, but once satisfied – once we have that career or position which gives us self-respect – the craving stops. We sit back and rest on our laurels. We stop moving forward and enjoy the outward recognition society affords us.

Those who go on to self-actualize, however, appreciate that the experience they have gathered is not an end in itself, but a stepping-stone to achieving their life's true purpose. To achieve self-actualization, they need to rip away the constraints which their satisfied self-esteem has put on their experience. Instead, this experience needs to be released and channeled towards solving the problems which are the person's life path.

This often feels counter-intuitive, because removing the constraints on experience requires a trait that is the very antithesis of the ego and self-esteem that led us to gather the experience in the first place. It takes humility. For only with humility can we appreciate the need to expose ourselves to the further learning that is necessary to open our minds. Only with humility can we accept that, despite all our experience, we know very little and hence have to open ourselves up to learning from people from other walks of life.

A friendship transcending social boundaries
Eleanor Roosevelt was born into the privilege of the Victorian era. Her family was, outwardly at least, the cream of East Coast society in the United States with her mother a society belle and her father a member of the most prestigious New York clubs. Both, however, were distant parents: one too beautiful to care about her plain daughter, the other a notorious alcoholic.

Eleanor spent part of her education in Europe, and this gave her an early exposure to the rich diversity of cultures that existed outside the society into which she was born. At nineteen years old, she accepted a marriage proposal from her distant cousin, Franklin Delano Roosevelt and her life's path as a wife and mother in an ambitious East Coast aristocratic family seemed set.

For the next thirteen years Eleanor played this part as best she could, supporting her husband's political career and subjugating herself to her mother-in-law. In 1918, however, the bottom fell out of Eleanor's world, when she discovered that Franklin had been having an affair with her friend, Lucy Mercer. Confronting Franklin with his infidelity, Eleanor offered him a divorce but the entire Roosevelt clan mobilized against this, knowing it would sound the death-knell for his political career.

Although Eleanor accepted the need to stay married for the sake of Franklin's ambitions, she made certain demands which led to a change in their relationship. Eleanor insisted on having her own separate life which centered on the cottage called Val-Kill in Hyde Park. She learned to drive and cook and started to widen her own circle of friends which existed outside of the society into which she was born.

Still, however, she remained a doting wife, both in outward appearance and in actuality. When Franklin became ill with polio in 1921, Eleanor stayed by his side, becoming his full-time carer, helping to bath him, shave him and administer his catheters. The way Roosevelt developed strength – together with a deeper appreciation of the fundamentals of life – from his predicament, made a deep impression on Eleanor. It re-built the strong admiration she had for him. It also gave her a strength and persistence that underpinned her character for the rest of her life.

Eleanor's experience led her to a position where, in a sense, she was living two different lives, each completely separate yet both entirely reconcilable. In public, she was Franklin's wife, their relationship the definition of propriety and devotion, underpinned by the fortitude from the difficulties which they had gone through. In private, however, Eleanor continued to develop her personal sphere of interests from her base in Val-Kill. These interests harked back to the appreciation of diversity she had acquired during her period of education in Europe and this mind-set soon emerged in a deeply-held passion for civil rights and an openness to those at all levels of society.

To her mother-in-law's horror, Eleanor fired all her existing servants and hired a household of black staff in their place. She became politically active in the League of Women Voters and other organizations, which was beyond the expectations of a politician's wife. When her husband became President, Eleanor redefined the role of First Lady writing her own newspaper column called 'My Day' and championing civil rights causes. Most of all, she engaged in correspondence with people of all levels of society, learning different viewpoints and about the deep social problems that needed to be solved.

One such correspondent was Pauli Murray, twenty-six years younger than Eleanor Roosevelt, and the granddaughter of a mulatto slave.[46] Murray was born in Baltimore, Maryland and lost both her parents at a young age, her father being murdered whilst a resident at an insane asylum. It was a tragedy that ignited a passion for justice in Murray and she threw herself into learning, graduating with a bachelor of arts in January 1933 from Hunter College. At the height of the Depression, however, having struggled to find a job, Murray fell ill. In 1935, she signed up for Camp Tera, one of the havens for the homeless and unemployed to emerge from the New Deal's Civilian Conservation Corp aiming to rebuild the health and morale of the unemployed.

It was at Camp Tera that Murray first encountered Eleanor Roosevelt when the First Lady visited. This was the type of visit the First Lady made as routine, exposing herself to all levels of society and making sure places such as Camp Tera were racially inclusive as she insisted they had to be. They did not speak at this time, Murray being too shy to lift her head from her book and Eleanor not wishing to disturb an avid reader.

Three years later, however, Murray lost her shyness and began a correspondence with Eleanor Roosevelt with an impassioned criticism of President Roosevelt's speech at the University of North Carolina (UNC), at which he had just accepted an honorary doctorate. Murray was angry at the contradiction between the President's description of UNC as a "liberal institution" and the fact that it still practiced segregation (and indeed had rejected her application to study there). The President's reticence contrasted sharply with his wife's activism a few weeks earlier at the Southern Conference for Human Welfare in Alabama. City officials were keen to ensure local segregation laws were complied with during the conference and when the First Lady sat down in the black section, the police asked her to move. To avoid making a scene, but at the same time not wishing to give up on a principle in which she fiercely believed, Eleanor Roosevelt moved her chair to the mid-way point between the black and white sections, a powerfully symbolic gesture of inclusiveness which left Murray deeply impressed.

So it was that Murray came to write to the First Lady, expressing her fury at her husband's approval of UNC. To Murray's surprise she received a personal response from the First Lady, agreeing with Murray's sentiments, but suggesting that the South would change gradually with time and that patience was needed. In particular, Eleanor pointed to the change in youth which was happening as being a hopeful sign, something that she found inspiring.

This was the first exchange in a life-long correspondence and friendship between Pauli Murray and Eleanor Roosevelt. Throughout it all, Murray's missives were filled with fiery passion, educating Eleanor on the day-to-day racial and women's rights issues she encountered, from a young black woman's viewpoint. Eleanor absorbed everything Murray told her and pushed to the limits what she could do within the confines of the political constraints in which she laboured as the President's wife. Her husband's power-base meant that going overtly against the southern states, which still practiced segregation, was impossible. Still, Eleanor pushed things to the boundaries, and sometimes beyond, whenever she could.

No better example of this exists than in the engagement Murray and Roosevelt had on the Odell Waller case between 1940 and 1942. Odell Waller was a twenty-three year-old black sharecropper from Virginia who had shot his white landlord when the landlord had refused to pay Waller for his share of the crop. Convicted of first degree murder by an all-white jury, Waller was on death row. Murray was recruited by the Workers Defense League as a field secretary to assist with raising funds for Waller's appeal and threw herself into her work with passion. She went on tour with Waller's mother, speaking in public about the plight of share-croppers and the limited recourse to justice available.

Murray wrote to Eleanor Roosevelt several times for help. Shackled by politics from doing anything publicly, Eleanor did what she could behind the scenes, personally forwarding Murray's correspondence to the governor of Virginia. She even prompted her husband, Franklin, to write to the governor informing him how he, the President, had once granted clemency in a death-row case when governor of New York. The Virginian governor ended up granting Waller a reprieve, but only so that the case could be reheard. At the new hearing, however, the original findings were upheld.

Murray then organized a delegation of civil rights leaders to go the White House to ask for a last-minute intervention. The President was taken up with other business, but Eleanor kept trying to interrupt her husband, until eventually he took her call. Franklin told his wife that he felt everything had been done and indeed that the governor had already re-heard the case and had decided it within his rights. The First Lady told the delegation that she had done everything she could possibly do. Every avenue had been exhausted. She could do no more.

Waller's execution was a hard blow for Murray to take, but it did inspire her to pursue a legal career which she did by entering Howard University. After her law degree, Murray applied to graduate school at Harvard, but the "all male" policy led to her rejection. She asked Eleanor for help and this prompted a letter from the President himself, but again the decision stood. Still, on her graduation from Howard, Pauli Murray was astonished to receive a bouquet of flowers from both Eleanor and Franklin.

Instead of Harvard, Murray went to Berkley, where she passed the bar exam in 1945. Her thesis was the first to be published by an African American woman in the law review as well as being the first on the subject of sex discrimination in employment.

As for Eleanor, partly to keep her from offending the South at a time of heightened racial tension, she was dispatched by her husband to go to visit troops abroad in 1943. Eleanor made a point of visiting African American troops on this trip and even shocked one nineteen-year-old soldier when she shared his ice-cream with him. It was a moment the soldier never forgot, and one which demonstrated, how far Eleanor Roosevelt had come in furthering the cause of civil rights with her disarming charm.

So it was that the two friends – Eleanor Roosevelt and Pauli Murray – from different sections of society, twenty-six years apart in age, had inspired each other to develop experiences that neither would have otherwise had. This was probably the moment in their lives when they reached Maslow's fourth level, satisfying their need for self-esteem. In later years, however, their mutual inspiration would lead them on to self-actualization and the discovery of their true purpose.

From friendship to self-actualization
In 1945, the whole nation mourned the death of President Franklin Delano Roosevelt, the man who had led them through the Great Depression and the Second World War. For Eleanor, her husband's passing meant an abrupt end to the title of First Lady which she had held since 1933. Instead of moving quietly into the obscurity of retirement, however, Eleanor took full advantage of the removal of the political constraints under which she had laboured in deference to her husband's position. For the rest of her life, she fought to further the rights of minorities, those in poverty and women across the world. In doing so, she realized her purpose, acquired a status that went far beyond her role as First Lady and became the living embodiment of self-actualization.

Eleanor's advocacy against isolationism brought home to the American people the dreadful dislocation in post-war Europe. She stressed how it was important for the United States not to live prosperously with blinkers on, when the world around her was in misery.[47] Her passion for international cooperation to solve the problems facing humanity, led to her appointment as the head of the UN Commission on Human Rights.

Domestically, too, Eleanor pushed civil rights wherever she could, becoming a board member of the NAACP and countless other organizations. In 1954, following the landmark Supreme Court decision in *Brown v. Board of Education*, which ended the concept of "separate but equal", on which segregation was based, she fought to see segregation ended wherever it was resisted. Rosa Parks, the seamstress and NAACP member, who was arrested for defying a request to move to the black section of a segregated bus, thereby sparking a mass boycott in Montgomery, was invited to tea by Eleanor in a public show of equality and support. When Autherine Lucy became the first black student to be admitted to the University of Alabama under a court order in 1955, only to be expelled for her own safety, Eleanor not only signed the petition for Lucy's reinstatement, but appeared with her at a civil rights rally in Madison Square Garden.[48] When, in 1957, President Eisenhower used the National Guard to allow black students entry to Little Rock Central High School, Eleanor called on Eisenhower to lead the students into the school himself to demonstrate that the principle of "equal but separate" no longer had any place in society. When President Kennedy, in 1961, set up his Commission on the Status of Women, Eleanor Roosevelt became the natural choice to be its head.

Throughout this entire period, the correspondence between Eleanor Roosevelt and Pauli Murray continued, inspiring them both to greater efforts on civil rights issues. Murray ran for New York City Council in 1949, encouraged by a donation from Eleanor. Although Murray did not win, she went on to become a distinguished legal scholar, with one of her essays being relied on by the NAACP's legal team in the *Brown v. Board of Education* case. In 1956, Murray unleashed her creative streak with the publication of *Proud Shoes*, a personal memoir which told the story of her family. Eleanor Roosevelt was so inspired by the memoir she quoted from it in her 'My Day' column, indicating that anyone interested in civil rights would find it a stimulating read.

By the time she passed away in 1962, Eleanor Roosevelt had emerged as a world beacon of diversity and liberalism. She had lived her life by these principles and moved civil rights causes to the forefront of the global agenda. At one stage, she had even been talked about as a possible candidate for being the first woman President, such was the immensity of her reputation. But the public moral positions she took and the humility with which she conducted herself throughout her life meant Eleanor

Roosevelt's impact on the world was very much more than any mere politician's would have been. She had truly emerged from her husband's shadow to become a key figure in her own right, particularly for her work in transforming women's position in society.

As for Pauli Murray, she went on to be the first African American to earn a doctorate in the science of law from Yale and a Professor at Brandeis University. Murray's path to true self-actualization, however, was achieved in 1977 when she became the first African American woman to be ordained into the priesthood of the Episcopalian Church. Her theological path gave her the moral foundation for which she had always been searching to tackle inequality. It was as if her legal training and creativity as a writer had been mere preparation for the pastoral role she performed to the end of her life.

Eleanor Roosevelt and reverse mentoring
Eleanor Roosevelt is one of the greatest women and human beings the world has seen. Her achievements emerge from her humility, a character trait so often absent today in a society which venerates the cult of personality. She took people as they came, spoke to them not as the First Lady but as a friend and was completely devoid of airs and graces.

On one occasion Murray took her niece to visit Eleanor. When they entered the living room, Eleanor was in deep conversation on world issues with Golda Meir, then the Israeli minister for foreign affairs, several Protestant leaders, and a female judge. After the meeting broke up and the dignitaries left, Murray's niece was astonished at the sight of the former First Lady emptying ashtrays, tidying up, and feeding cookies to her Scottish terrier.[49] This summed up Eleanor Roosevelt's attitude to the world and the power of her natural humility. She felt that she was no better than anybody else, and because of this, she was interested in everybody else.

It was her humility which enabled Eleanor Roosevelt to be inspired by people from all walks of life, including Pauli Murray. The reverse-mentoring dynamic which was present in this unlikely friendship between the former First Lady and the grand-daughter of a mulatto slave was shown in an article Eleanor Roosevelt wrote for the 1953 issue of *Ebony* entitled, 'Some of My Best Friends Are Negro'. In it, Eleanor cited Murray as a friend who was a charming young woman lawyer and a bit of a "firebrand".[50] Murray was thrilled with this depiction and possibly saw the influence her friendship was having, when, in October 1956, an impassioned speech by Eleanor Roosevelt, in support of Adlai Stevenson's presidential campaign, caused Murray to write to the former First Lady and tell her she was a firebrand herself.[51]

Indeed Eleanor Roosevelt was and the world is a much better place for it.

Chapter 10

THE ART OF CONSTANT STUDY

It's the beginning of my final year at university, the last in a four-year course. Everything rests on the eight three-hour final exams that happen in June, ten months down the road. Ten months seems a long way away at the outset of the academic year. Ten months in which I can study, learn, plan, revise, go through countless mock timed-essays and review past papers to perfect my exam technique. I feel like an athlete going into training for the Olympics, honing my knowledge, getting myself ready to peak during that crucial two week period in the summer. That will be when it really matters. There will be no "repeats". How I perform in my final exams will dictate the course of the rest of my life. It's make or break, the path to success or the road to failure.

Suddenly, someone pushes the fast-forward button. It's as if I'm watching a film of those ten months flashing by at speed and there's nothing I can do to hit pause or slow things down. Figures with helium-pitch voices rapidly squiggle in and out of the screen. When the play button is hit again, the film ends and here I am, sitting at a desk with hundreds of others in a massive, sterile hall. The slow tick of the clock on the wall offers the only sound.

Somehow it's June already and this is the first day of my exams. No, it can't be. The panic begins to rise as I realize I know nothing. Worse than that, I feel I haven't slept in the last ten months. It's like I'm moving through quick-sand. I'm struggling even to lift the pen from the desk, it weighs a ton. Try as a might, I cannot shift its deadweight, until the moment the invigilator pipes up with his best Eminem impression.

"The Clock's run out. Times up. Over. Pow."

And it is. My life is over. How am I going to face my parents, my friends, myself?

That's when I wake up, drenched in sweat, my heart pounding against the walls of my panic-filled chest. It takes me a few minutes to snap back to reality. The bed-side clock tells me its 3am, my aching back reassures me I'm in my forties. I look over at my wife in bed next to me asleep. Her presence brings the sweet elixir of relief, because it means two decades have passed since my finals, thank God! This was just another of those anxiety-laced nightmares that happen every so often.

I don't know why I get these dreams, but every six months or so a version of this nightmare visits me and it's horrible. The thing is, I didn't do too badly in my finals, so it makes little sense. But every time I wake up and realize it was just a dream, I still give thanks about that period of my life being over. There are no more exams for me, I reassure myself.

And in that moment I tell myself what is perhaps the most stupid thing in the world: I never have to study again.

The experience of study

You see, here's another problem with experience. It conditions our minds into linear thinking about our lives. We divide life into phases. Each phase is a key stepping-stone to acquiring the experience we need to move forward to the next phase. Once completed, however, a phase is never to be repeated (at least that's what we believe). Going back and doing a phase again is a waste of time. It's an admission of failure, in fact. So, one after the other, we move through the phases of our life: school, university, first job, second job, promotion, promotion, recognition. Once a phase is done, we put it on our CV and only look back on it with nostalgia to tell the story of how we got to where we are, but we never dream of delving back into it as a means of broadening our prospects for the future.

This is particularly true of the academic stage of our lives. Education and study is something we do when we are young, before we release ourselves onto the world to put what we learned into practice. Then, when we start work, progress and forward momentum rely on acquiring experience, playing politics and moving up the ladder. The more experienced we become, the better we are at playing the game and the higher up we move.

I've already mentioned the complacency which sets in, the deeper our experience becomes. How experience creates this natural tendency for us to look only at what we already know, to address the new problems presented to us. Sometimes this dynamic can be so dangerous that we blind ourselves to problems. For example, we might fail to see clinging on to a particular process for too long as a problem, because our experience tells us that's the way we've always done things.

As we move up the ladder of success, this sense of complacency turns into something far more dangerous and pernicious. It turns into arrogance. Arrogance born of experience tells us we are right and everyone else is wrong. It prevents us from listening to other opinions, unless those opinions agree with our own. Our minds close and we become hostile to those whose ideas are fresh and worth exploring.

Most dangerous of all, arrogance born of experience informs us that there is nothing new for us to learn. It lulls us into thinking that the peak of our experience is the outer limit of progress. We can develop no more and anyone who seeks to change us or what we have done is our enemy.

As you read these words, you may think "that's not me." But have you ever come out of a training course at work and thought "what a waste of time"? Have you ever groaned with dismay, when your company announces yet another new training initiative? These instinctive reactions to proposed change are the manifestation of arrogance brought on by experience. This is our experience telling us we don't need to learn, we don't need to change, we don't want to progress.

No-one is immune from this. It's part of the psychological make-up of human nature. Indeed, one of the clearest examples of this psychological dynamic can be found in the relationship between perhaps the two most famous psychoanalysts who ever lived.

Carl Jung and Sigmund Freud

Early on his career, Carl Jung began working with the mentally ill, pioneering a new treatment based on word association. He used this to understand his patients' subconscious thoughts and developed the theory of the psychological complex, a core pattern of highly-charged emotions, stimulated around a common theme in the subconscious of an individual. In 1906, when he was thirty years old, Jung sent his research to the leading psychologist in the world at the time, Sigmund Freud. Freud was twenty years Jung's senior and had already achieved fame and recognition for his pioneering work on the unconscious mind, based on his sexual theories. Finding Jung's work of interest, Freud exchanged some of his own research in return.

The two men met face-to-face for the first time at Freud's home in 1907 and there was an immediate intellectual connection between them. They spent that day locked in thirteen hours of deep conversation, exploring their mutual ideas on the human mind. Soon after this, Freud came to view Jung as his intellectual heir apparent, and the older man began playing mentor to his younger protégé. In 1909, they travelled to the United States together and attended a conference at Clarke University which marked a watershed in the acceptance of psychoanalysis in North America. With Freud's endorsement, Jung's career quickly advanced and he became life chairman of the International Psychoanalytical Association.

In 1910, however, the relationship turned sour. The catalyst for this was when Freud asked Jung very directly never to abandon his sexual theories. "That is the most essential thing of all. You see, we must make a dogma of it, an unshakeable bulwark."[52] Jung was disturbed by this request, which went against the continued development and new discoveries on which every science is based. Freud, nearing the end of his career, appeared more intent on the preservation of his influence, legacy and reputation than continuing the quest for exploration which had originally driven him in his early years and which underpinned his intellectual friendship with Jung. The request was especially disturbing for Jung as his own research was leading him increasingly to diverge from Freud's theory, by placing less emphasis on sexual motives and more on spiritual development as a key driver of the unconscious mind.

Upset by the different direction Jung's research was taking, Freud began to ridicule Jung's work as occultism. The final break between the two men came when Freud very deliberately slighted Jung in 1913, by visiting Jung's colleague, Ludwig Binswanger in Kreuzlingen, instead of visiting Jung. So strongly did Jung feel about this intended insult, that he forever referred to it as the Kreuzlingen gesture.

Freud's public break with Jung proved disastrous for Jung's career as his latest publication was declared by his former mentor to be the work of a mystic. Jung felt forced to resign every position he had obtained with Freud's support, including his chairmanship of the International Psychoanalytical Association. His consequent isolation, loss of status in academic circles, and professional extradition at the hands of Freud led Jung into the depths of a fully-blown personal mid-life crisis.

In Freud's ruin of Jung's career, we see, fully exposed, the dangerous limits of experience. The status Freud had achieved by the twilight of his career appeared to manifest itself in an intellectual arrogance that led him to refuse to see beyond the theories he had developed and which had gained him his reputation. Keen to preserve his intellectual legacy, Freud became hell-bent on stopping his protégé from seeking to take his theories in a different but more progressive direction.

Yet in crisis comes opportunity, and from the personal crisis which Jung experienced, emerged some of his most influential work, which not only matched Freud's but overtook it. Taking refuge in childlike play for comfort, Jung found building toy castles and towers as a means of restoring himself to a place of calm. This self-therapy led to his pioneering work in art therapy for persons suffering a brain injury. Further, the painful self-analysis which Jung forced himself through led him to develop an understanding of psychological types, such as introverts and extroverts, categories which are still used to this day in the Myers-Briggs personality test, which has been adopted by businesses across the world. In the depths of his crisis, Jung also lapsed further into spiritualism and this led to him perfecting his research on the subconscious, arguing that it was affected as much by a person's own past experiences as by the sexual dynamic which Freud had found. Jung's theories on the subconscious are now commonly accepted by the psychoanalyst industry and have led to millions being helped through therapy.

Despite Freud's efforts to stop it from happening, Jung took his mentor's theories to the next level. Unlike Freud, who had let arrogance born from his experience constrain his thinking, Carl Jung had been forced through crisis to a place of abject humility and a mindset which released his experience to further exploration.

So what can we learn from the relationship between Sigmund Freud and Carl Jung?

Firstly, in Freud, we see how experience can breed arrogance, that most pernicious of characteristics. For those with experience, arrogance is the easy default option. It is the cool bully in the playground wearing a leather jacket and sporting tattoos, disparaging anyone who dares to be diligent or shows any sign of wanting to learn something new. Humility, however, is the road less-travelled, a trait which those with much experience find completely counter-intuitive. It's the bully's good classmate who, like Carl Jung, is ready to risk humiliation by standing up to the bully and telling him to back off when he's picking on the runtiest kid with milk-bottle glasses. Sure the good classmate may take some transient flack from the bully for doing this, but that's all it will be. In the long run, the bully will end up as the loser, as the good classmate goes on to greater things. So, pay attention! Arrogance stops us wanting to learn more, but humility makes us lifelong learners.

Secondly, we see that learning is very much more than academic study alone. The activities to which Carl Jung felt himself drawn in his personal crisis, became the very things he learned from to develop the theories which still have relevance to this day. Through enforced humility, Jung came to see the value in everything he did and used it to change to the world. So never underestimate the most mundane of tasks, for even these provide a learning experience. For Jung, building sandcastles led to his pioneering work in art therapy. For you – who knows? – hours spent at the photocopier may build resilience, and proof-reading can develop your eye for detail.

Thirdly, we learn how humility is the pathway to opening up one's experience to be used for progress. Humility says to us: we must always keep ourselves open to learning from others, especially those younger than ourselves who see the world differently. In this way, a humble outlook is key to reverse mentoring.

Those who are humble enough to accept, that no matter how much experience we have, we should never stop learning from those younger than ourselves, can achieve great leaps of progression. Sometimes, as was the case with

Jung, it takes an extreme crisis or event in our lives to bring us to this place of humility. Indeed, perhaps there was an element of crisis at work in me when my young cousin Anthony passed away (see Chapter 3), or when Napoleon was sent into exile and humiliation on St Helena where he met Betsy Balcombe (see Chapter 5). Yet crisis does not have to be a pre-requisite for learning this lesson. Those who adopt humility from a place of strength and experience, rather than crisis, can become life-long learners and make a big impact in the world.

Benjamin Franklin and Polly Stevenson

In Benjamin Franklin, one of the founding fathers of the United States of America, we find perhaps the pinnacle exemplar of a devotee to life-long learning. Certainly in Franklin's early years, studying came naturally to him. He was a young man in a hurry to make his way in the world and saw the acquisition of knowledge as the path to success.

As an apprentice at his brother's print-shop, he would immerse himself in books, staying up into the early hours of the morning reading anything he could get his hands on. He was particularly taken with John Bunyan's *Pilgrim's Progress*, at the heart of which lay the message that human progress depended on a steady increase in knowledge and wisdom. He also engaged in perfecting his ability to debate by disputing issues of the day with his fellow apprentice John Collins. Together, they would sharpen their skills by taking different sides on a subject and thrashing it out.

Unlike many, however, who start out in their youth with good intentions, but whose enthusiasm fades away in later years, Benjamin Franklin was able to keep up his learning habit throughout the entire course of his long life (he died at the age of eighty-four). Why was this?

One of the main reasons was because, unlike Sigmund Freud, Franklin avoided ever becoming entrapped by arrogance. This can, perhaps, be put down to a famous incident in his youth which taught Franklin the value of avoiding arrogance at all costs. Early on in his life Franklin knew he wanted to be a writer. To hone his skills, he would study essays in the *Spectator* magazine, then attempt to re-write them in his own style. In this way he was able to develop the conversational and witty writing voice for which he would later become famous. To further test his abilities, when he was sixteen and still apprenticed to his brother James, Franklin decided to seek publication of his work. He knew that neither his brother's print shop nor any other publisher would accept the work of a mere teenager. So instead, disguising his handwriting, Franklin wrote a series of fourteen humorous essays in the name of a fictional prudish widow by the name of Silence Dogood. Franklin delivered the essays anonymously to his brother James's printing press at night. So impressed was James with their quality, that they were duly published in the *Courant* in 1722. The essays quickly became popular for the witty observations on key issues of the day which they offered.

The acclaim pleased Franklin and – swept up with a rush of vanity – he revealed himself to James as the true author. Rather than receiving praise from his older brother, however, he was chastised for his deception. Further, from then on, James went out of his way to make sure his younger brother knew his place as a mere apprentice, subjecting him to the occasional beating and generally making him aware of his inferiority.

So it was that Benjamin Franklin quickly learned the dangers of giving in to feelings of vanity. He realized that self-aggrandizement could easily ignite jealously and deep-seated arrogance in others, as it had done in his brother James, which could only prove harmful to himself. Instead, Franklin learned there was value in maintaining humility and focusing solely on the work in front of him, which he proceeded to do. From that moment on, he set aside any desire for recognition and acclaim, in favour of hard work and performing good works for their own sake. It was an approach that led to Benjamin Franklin having remarkable success and it touched every area of his life.

With this renewed focus and industry, Franklin was able to open his own publishing house and built it into a successful business. So much so, in fact, that he was able to retire, financially secure, by the age of forty-two. Instead of resting on his laurels, however, and living a life of luxury and leisure, Franklin rigorously continued to pursue learning and research, particularly in the subject of science, for which he had a considerable passion. His pioneering work on electricity and snatching lightning from the sky with a child's kite, helped usher in a scientific revolution. His parlour trick of stilling a rippling pond with a flick of his walking stick (which released an unseen drop of oil) led to the saying, "pouring oil on troubled waters".[53]

As a writer too, Franklin's self-deprecating and witty humour quickly became popular and won him considerable fame. Building on the success of his Silence Dogood letters, he wrote *Poor Richard's Almanac*, replete with maxims of wisdom still used to this day (for example, "Early to bed and early to rise, makes a man healthy, wealthy and wise"). Further, his autobiography has been called, probably the first self-help book ever to be published.[54]

It is, however, as a politician that Benjamin Franklin is mainly remembered. The debate style he cultivated in the practice he developed with fellow apprentice John Collins during his youth certainly stood him in good stead. Always coming at his opponent cloaked in humility, Franklin would feign a lack of knowledge to ask innocent questions which would subtly draw his opponent into concessions that would eventually prove his point. This was diplomacy at its best and Franklin deployed it with great skill in his negotiations with the French during the war of independence. His skilled oratory before the British Parliament on the Stamp Act also won him considerable credit. Furthermore, the contributions he made to the principles on which the United States was founded, as recorded in the Declaration of Independence and its Constitution, place Benjamin Franklin in the pantheon of history as one of the founding fathers.

To all of Benjamin Franklin's accolades there is another considerable achievement we can add: that of a pioneer in the field of reverse mentoring. The humility he adopted kept his mind open to learn, especially from those younger than himself. Indeed, throughout his life, Franklin made it a practice to befriend younger people – women in particular – forging relationships with them as if they were his children. His relationship with Polly Stevenson, the daughter of his landlady whom he met in London, is a case in point.[55] The letters he wrote to Polly were full of instruction on life and morals as well as science and education. He recommended books for her to read and tutored her on philosophy. In return, she delighted him with her constant questions and discourse which showed him how her mind worked and kept him intellectually stimulated.

In his relationship with Polly Stevenson, we see Benjamin Franklin using reverse mentoring to great effect. Firstly, by passing on his own experience Franklin afforded himself the opportunity of reflecting and exploring more deeply the knowledge he had already learned, ensuring it remained active and always easily accessible. Secondly, by exposing himself to the youthful mind of others, he was able to feed off their enthusiasm and keep his own mind youthful, open and hence productive. Thirdly, by looking at the world through the youthful eyes of others, he was able to keep his mind full of the childlike curiosity which was the key to his inventiveness.

Benjamin Franklin was able to do this because he never allowed his vast experience to trap him within its limits. He never let himself be held back by arrogance. Instead, through the deliberate adoption of humility, he kept his mind curious and open to the very end and when his curiosity became mixed with his experience, it left a cocktail that extended the boundaries of human knowledge, even late on in his life. Indeed, Franklin is credited with suggesting Daylight Savings time and one of his most famous inventions – bifocal glasses – when he was in his seventies.

So it is that Benjamin Franklin, with his commitment to humility, life-long learning and child-like curiosity, stands as one of the most successful examples of reverse mentoring the world has ever seen.

Learning by teaching

We see then in the example of Benjamin Franklin, how humility is the key ingredient to reverse mentoring. Not only does humility underpin our continual desire for learning by making us recognise there is always more for us to learn, it also removes the limitations which arrogance places on the sources of our learning, by opening us up to the possibility that we can learn from someone younger and with considerably less experience than ourselves. Furthermore, humility creates equality between the mentor and protégé. It is equality which makes the reverse mentoring relationship a two-way street, where the participants can both teach and learn at the same time.

This last element begs further exploration. Reverse mentoring works because it throws together two minds from different generations and backgrounds in a situation of equality. Both experienced mentor and inexperienced protégé are learners, but equally and just as importantly, both are teachers. Benjamin Franklin did not just listen to Polly Stevenson. He engaged in vibrant discourse with her and taught her lessons from his own experience. We see this in the letters he wrote, where he recommended books for her to read and passed on his philosophy.

This dynamic of being a teacher is as key to reverse mentoring as it is to traditional mentoring. Not only does it enable the mentor to deepen his understanding of a subject he already knows about, but – by exposing such knowledge to questioning by someone younger than himself – the mentor also opens up his knowledge for further development. In other words, through reverse mentoring, teaching becomes a way of learning.

Think of it this way. Many professions require their practitioners to complete a certain minimum number of study hours every year to keep their knowledge up to date. This is entirely laudable. Professionals should keep their skills current and honed. Often these hours are completed through lectures held towards the end of the day, so the attending practitioners can go home or catch up on the latest gossip over a drink or two afterwards. This, however, means that these lectures become a matter of form over substance, where the purpose of passing on substantive knowledge is secondary to the need to tick a compliance box and arrange a social gathering.

Part of the problem lies in the lecturing process itself. It is a highly inefficient means of transferring knowledge. By this stage in their careers, professionals understand this and hence pay lecturing scant respect. In the 1960s, the National Training Laboratories (NTL) Institute in Bethel, Maine, developed a piece of research known as "the Learning Pyramid",[56] which compared different methods of learning to try to find which was the best in terms of achieving the aim of learning, namely knowledge transfer and a deeper understanding of the subject matter. According to the Learning Pyramid, sitting in a lecture is by far the most inefficient learning method, as students retain only five percent of what they hear. So it is that all professionals sitting in a lecture are effectively wasting their time. That is, except those professionals who go back to their offices to teach others what they have learned. The simple of act of teaching someone else the subject matter, according to the Learning Pyramid, actually leads to retention of ninety-five percent of the information by the teacher.

The clear lesson here is that teaching a subject, is by far the best mechanism for learning and understanding it. In a lecture attended by professionals, the professional who learns the most is the one at the front doing all the talking. Why? It's the fear factor at play. If you are going to expose yourself like that and open yourself up publicly to questioning, you are going to make damn sure you're on top of your subject matter.

Furthermore, through the mechanism of teaching, not only do you deepen your understanding of the topic, if you are able to keep your mind open and curious, you are also able to evolve the topic beyond its limits. And those in a position to teach a topic have at their disposal the best resource to keep their minds open, curious and critical about their topic: their students. Students, especially those from a different generation to their teacher, can bring, to an existing subject, refreshing and new viewpoints every day. By exposing themselves to these different viewpoints, great teachers can remove the limits on their own understanding of a subject and develop it further.

Freddie Roach, the famous boxing coach, is a great example of this dynamic in action. After his career in the ring ended, Freddie started to hang around the gym run by the legendary boxing trainer, Eddie Futch, Freddie's former coach.[57] Like many boxers, Freddie missed the thrill of going toe-to-toe in the ring with another fighter. He soon found a way of recapturing that feeling by helping Futch's fighters work out. For this Freddie would put on those large padded mitts trainers use, jump in the ring, and let fighters go to work perfecting their punches.

Freddie, however, took mitt-work to a far higher level. In fact, he used it to evolve an entirely new way of training. He would spend time studying a fighter's next opponent, then he would put on the mitts, get in the ring and replicate how the opponent would fight. He would work with the fighter on developing a strategy to beat the opponent, enabling the fighter to deploy his strengths effectively and exploit the opponent's weaknesses.

Soon, using this innovative method, Freddie began developing a reputation as a trainer himself and he left Futch's gym to branch out on his own. His revolutionary way of training with the mitts attracted many up and coming fighters to his door. One day, in walked a fighter from the Philippines called Manny Pacquiao, who was looking for a trainer in the United States to get him to the next level. Many trainers had already watched Manny work out and taken a pass. Watching wasn't how Freddie trained, however. He put on the mitts and got into the ring with Manny. From the speed and raw power of Manny's first punch, Freddie knew he had someone special and agreed to train him.

The coach-fighter relationship blossomed, as Freddie – through his mitt-work – transformed Manny into a multi-dimensional fighter. This was made easy by Manny's ability to absorb everything Freddie taught. Manny wasn't like other fighters in Freddie's stable who, as they got a bit of success under their belt, grew an arrogance that made them think they knew best and led them to stop listening to Freddie. The careers of these other fighters would quickly plateau as they reached the limits of their ability. Manny, by contrast, was humble. He just kept on absorbing, listening, learning, improving and most importantly, winning.

After a while, Manny started to open up in his mitt-work routines with Freddie. He started to provide his own suggestions, which Freddie was open-minded enough to take on board. One day, during a mitt-work session, Manny improvised a move where he ducked and came at Freddie from an angle. Freddie was in awe. He told Manny to try it again, so Manny did. "Wow!" thought Freddie. So impressed was Freddie by the move, he used it to develop a whole new style of fighting for Manny, which kept opponents from working out how he would fight. Freddie, as teacher, had taken his ability to coach to a higher level because he was open-minded enough to let Manny teach him. Through teaching, Freddie had let himself be taught and as a result became even better.

With Freddie in his corner, Manny Pacquiao went on to become one of the best fighters of his generation. Freddie Roach has emerged indisputably as one of the best coaches of all time, because he never closed his mind to learning from his fighters. Their training relationship offers one of the best modern-day examples of the power of reverse mentoring.

This same extraordinary teacher/student reverse mentoring dynamic we see at work between Metallica lead guitarist Kirk Hammett and his instructor Joe Satriani.[58] Whilst many lead-guitarists would have seen joining Metallica as the peak of their profession, the first thing Hammett did after signing on was go out and find Satriani, the best guitar instructor in the business, to teach him. As a teacher, Satriani was no pushover. He put Hammett through two years of weekly tuition, critiquing his style and drilling him in music theory. Hammett put away his ego and just learned. The result? Hammett went onto become one of the greats on the metal scene. But that's only half the story. Joe Satriani, in teaching guitar, absorbed new things from his students and combined it with his own considerable experience to become a virtuoso, with no less than six gold and platinum discs under his belt.

The reverse mentoring recipe
We can see in the examples in this chapter the key ingredients that make a reverse mentoring relationship successful.

Humility is perhaps the key ingredient and it's the most difficult trait to master, especially for those with experience. The more experience we acquire, the more we have a tendency to tell ourselves how great we are. How we know everything already. How we don't need to listen to anyone else. Experience and arrogance are natural bedfellows, but arrogance is the most dangerous of character traits. It stops us from developing.

Where arrogance prevents us from learning, humility opens up our minds. Humility makes us appreciate how much more there is for us to learn and creates in us a burning desire to improve. Humility makes us realize, that the more we know, the more there is that we don't know. Humility keeps us curious and makes us life-long learners, just like it did with Benjamin Franklin.

Equality between mentor and protégé is another key ingredient and it emerges from humility. Arrogance makes us think we are superior. Humility makes us realize we are anything but. It creates in us an appreciation that we have something that we can learn from our reverse-mentor, and makes us open-minded enough to do so. Equality makes us listeners and not just talkers.

The third key ingredient is the value of learning through teaching. Teaching and learning become one and the same thing in a reverse mentoring relationship. Through the mechanism of teaching we deepen our understanding of a subject, for nothing makes us know a subject more than having to teach it. Couple this with humility and equality, we find that, through teaching, we open our experience up to critique by someone coming at us from a different viewpoint. This is the recipe for innovation. Freddie Roach invented a completely new way of boxing, because Manny Pacquiao came at him from an angle in one of his mitt-work sessions. Freddie had already pioneered mitt-work as an entirely new training method, but he took things to another level when using it to train Manny. Through teaching, Freddie learned from his protégé. Both became the best at what they did, because they were humble enough to realize they needed each other to learn more.

Humility, equality, and teaching to learn; these three ingredients are the keys to releasing the true power of reverse mentoring.

Chapter 11

THE SUMMER OF 1997

The premise of the essays in this book is, that whilst gaining experience provides the path to improvement and development, it also comes with significant drawbacks. Over-reliance on experience can hold back creative innovation and provide an enabler for existing methods to endure well past their sell-by date; in some instances, to the point where they become destructive.

We see this process most in the business context when a new methodology or theory comes to the fore. The business which first creates the method or theory and the consequent first adopters of it, gain significant first-mover advantage and march ahead of their competitors. This is fair enough, the reward for the risk they take by trying something new. Good on them, the world screams!

Soon, however, the competition plays catch-up. Often this is done by competitors buying in the experience from the early-adopters, hiring away their talent at significant cost, with the express remit to repeat for their new employer what they did for their old employer. "What you did there, I am paying you to do here", is how this simplistic human resources model works. By this means the new methodology is replicated across the industry, until it has changed from being the innovative shift in paradigm it once was, to the established standard procedure it now is.

Further, in the process of extending the methodology across an entire industry, it becomes standardized, since a one-size-fits-all model is easier apply. But through the process of standardization, often, the innovative dynamism that initially made the methodology such a significant paradigm shift is blunted, if not lost altogether.

This is when the experience of those early innovators, who by this stage have risen to the top of the industry, becomes counterproductive if not downright dangerous. The success these decision-makers gained from their "once innovative, now standard" methodology, coupled with the natural aging process, means they fail to see anything beyond it. Indeed they view its continued adoption, standardization and application across their industry, as proof of its continued relevance and modernity.

So it is that years pass by without the methodology ever being challenged. New generations of employees are trained in it, without even knowing the reason for its relevance. When they question it, the answer comes back, "That's the way we've always done it, so it must be right." That's the moment when those who are sitting at the top of their profession, those who once championed innovation, now serve as a barrier to change. The sad thing is, it's the experience which got them to the top in the first place which is now providing the blinkers.

At best, this process of innovation, fast adoption, standardization, and then resistance to reinvention, can lead to a once vibrant industry dying a natural death, as it is overtaken by other fields of endeavour in which true innovation remains alive and well. It is, one might say, just part and parcel of the macro business Darwinian environment. At worst, however, the process which venerates continuing with things well past their sell-by-date can lead to a crisis, reaching well beyond the industry which adopts it. In short, this dynamic can ruin people's lives.

The Global Financial Crisis – the definition of experience repeating itself

There is no more relevant example of this in modern history, than the Global Financial Crisis. The financial innovation leap here was mortgage-backed securitization, the mechanism by which the most standard financial instrument in the world – the household mortgage loan – was transformed into a financial time-bomb that exploded the world economy in September 2008.

Essentially through the mechanism of securitization, the most plain vanilla financial instruments known to us all – humble bank mortgages – were bundled up by their thousands and sold to capital market investors as bonds. The bond investors would thereby get their capital repaid over time with interest from the repayments made on the mortgage loans packaged up in the bonds. If, however, any mortgage borrower included in the bond defaulted on their mortgage loan, investors would lose the equivalent amount in their bond repayments.

In this early conception, securitization was an example of financial innovation at its best, a medium which brought together unconnected parts of the industry to solve several key problems. Primarily, securitization took the default risk associated with any particular mortgage loan which the bank faced, and spread it around thousands of investors, thereby making the risk of the few those of the many. This in turn enabled banks to make more mortgage loans, so that average families could get on the property ladder. By this mechanism people were lifted out of poverty and communities were built.

Secondly, it filled a hole in the capital market investment appetite created by the era of low interest rates. Pension funds and insurance companies' profits were being hit with the yield on government treasuries being so low, but their risk appetite limited them from investing too much in equities which were known for their volatility. What was needed was an investment with a risk profile that fit somewhere between the complete safety of government treasuries and the volatility of equities, so institutional investors could plug the gap. It was into this gap that the mortgage-backed security fit, and money flowed in like water.

As the demand for mortgage-backed securities thundered ahead, the process of standardization and scalability went into overdrive. Firstly, we saw this in the move from over-the-counter securities contracts negotiated deal by deal, to standardized contracts where all terms and conditions were set as standard, save for the price, which allowed for instantaneous deals to be struck. Secondly, we saw it in the massive replication in the types of mortgage-backed securities, as the same basic concept morphed into other financial instruments, which looked different, but which were basically the same, such as the collateralized debt obligation (CDO) and credit default swap (CDS).

Both CDOs and CDSs appeared at first to be financial innovations in their own right, but they were in fact the simple mortgage-backed security taken to the next level, aiming to diversify risk even further across the capital markets. Soon, however, things started to turn.

The investment bankers, who had invented these instruments, failed to see beyond them as a means of making money, and continued to replicate them, rather than looking for new innovations. In doing so, they turned the whole concept of securitization on its head. Originally, securitization had been a tool to enable banks to make more loans to people, by enabling the risk, associated with the occasional unavoidable default, to be diversified. The continued explosion of the securitization market, however, changed this dynamic such that, in order to keep up with the demand, banks – through aggressive sales tactics and lax underwriting standards – virtually forced mortgage loans down the throats of people who, based on their income status, would never have any chance of repaying them. This in turn introduced massive risk into the financial system without anyone seeing it because the plain vanilla mortgage continued to be viewed as safe (something confirmed by the rating agencies in the triple A (AAA) ratings they assigned).

Furthermore, instead of diversifying this massive increase in the risk of default across the capital markets, it ended up concentrating the risk on a few players. This was achieved by the repackaging of mortgage-backed securities into CDOs then CDO squareds and then CDSs. This wasn't innovation. Rather, it was the replication of past experience dressed up as innovation.

An institutional investor, sitting on these instruments in their portfolio, thought it had a diversified mix of risk exposure with different mortgages backing each security they held. Instead, however, it was just the same mortgages being recycled through different instruments. What should have been a pyramid cascading risk from the few to the many, entirely reversed itself, by funneling the massive risk which had been channeled to the many back down to the few, who were simply passing the same risk around themselves.

Inevitably, the whole thing came crashing down in September 2008, when the players on whom the risk was concentrated stopped playing altogether and tried to guess which one of them was sitting at the top of this spiral. Lehman Brothers, it was thought, provided the answer when it filed for bankruptcy on 15 September 2008. However, with Lehmans going down, the risk was passed back to the next player in the pyramid, in this instance, the global insurance organization AIG (American International Group). Realizing that if AIG went down, the risk would just be passed on to the next layer, until the whole financial system collapsed, the US government stepped in with a bail-out of US$85 billion in taxpayers' money to halt things there. But not even this could stop the global financial crisis which followed.

In the aftermath, everyone blamed the bankers and their financial wizardry of securitization which had blown up the system. This, however, is wrong. It wasn't the innovation of securitization itself which brought down the system, but the complete and utter failure of the system to innovate beyond securitization once it had become standardized and the experienced norm. What had brought us a successful experience in the past, it was thought, would continue to do so in the future. The blinkers of experience were to blame, and the younger generation, whose ideas could perhaps have shaken things up, are the ones who suffered.

When experience fails

The Global Financial Crisis in 2008 was not the first time we have seen this happen. The same dynamic afflicted the London insurance industry in the 1980s and 1990s.

Lloyd's of London is one of the most famous insurance institutions in the world. From its humble roots in the seventeenth century, as a coffee house where underwriters met to insure Britain's burgeoning marine trade, Lloyd's has grown into a globally-renowned sophisticated insurance organization with the capacity to manage practically any risk, no matter its size or complexity.

Lloyd's reputation is built on the solid foundation of good faith, or *uberrimae fidei*, the legal principle on which all insurance contracts are based. This was epitomized by the cable sent by Cuthbert Heath, a titan of the Lloyd's market at the turn of the twentieth century, in which he instructed his American agent to, "pay all our policyholders in full irrespective of the terms of their policies,"[59] in the wake of the 1906 San Francisco earthquake.

Lloyd's has also made its name through financial innovation, by constantly reinventing and stretching the humble insurance policy into new iterations, slicing and dicing risk, commoditizing catastrophe and spreading it across its large capital base. Through such innovation, Lloyd's transfers the catastrophic losses of the few around and around so that it eventually becomes borne by the many. This insurance dynamic of spreading risk in which the Lloyd's market specializes, enables whole societies to recover when disaster strikes, thereby making the unbearable slightly more bearable.

The excess-of-loss reinsurance contract was one such innovation, which was pioneered at Lloyd's for risk-spreading purposes. Here's how it works. An insurance company which specializes in homeowner's insurance will issue thousands of insurance policies protecting homeowners against the risk of property damage. Each insurance policy might cost a policyholder US$2,500 in premium per year, but in return the insurer commits to reimburse the homeowner for property damage loss up to, say, a limit of US$100,000 during that annual period. If the insurer has issued twenty thousand such policies, this means it would have collected US$50 million in premium (US$2,500 x 20,000).[60]

The probability is that the losses the insurer will have to pay out in the year under the policies will not exceed the US$50 million it has collected in premium. Most homeowner insurance claims are, after all, for minor losses like damage caused by a washing-machine flood, or leaky windows after a rain storm. Based on actuarial analysis, the insurer would have calculated that the US$50 million it has collected in premium is enough to pay these attritional losses and leave a tidy profit left over at the end of the year.

That said, the possibility that its losses will exceed US$50 million cannot be completely discounted. After all, the insurer's total potential liability under all twenty thousand policies is US$2 billion (US$100,000 limit x 20,000), so if its actuarial analysis is wrong, it could easily result in insolvency. By way of example, the insurer's losses could exceed US$50 million, if a number of the houses it insured all got hit at once by an unlikely catastrophe, like an earthquake.

As such, in order to protect against the improbable eventuality of a catastrophe, the insurer buys for itself insurance (called reinsurance) from other insurers. So the insurer might retain the first US$45 million in exposure under the policies it has issued, but then pay US$5 million in premium to reinsure all loss it has to pay in excess of

US$45 million with four reinsurers (who receive US$1.2 million each). This is known as "excess of loss" reinsurance because the reinsurers agree to pay loss in excess of the loss retained by the insurer.

The premium from the reinsurance as a percentage of the total exposure being reinsured is reduced when compared with the premium charged by the insurer to the homeowners, because the reinsurance only starts to pay out when the insurer's losses hit US$45 million, and the probability of losses ever reaching this level is relatively low. At this stage, then, the potential of catastrophic loss is spread by the mechanism of excess of loss reinsurance, to both the primary insurer and its four excess of loss reinsurers.

Each of the four excess reinsurers may in turn retain a portion of the risk they have reinsured, but then reinsure the rest with five reinsurers each. Again the amount of premium they pay is reduced, because the chances of a catastrophic loss exceeding both the combined retention of the primary insurer and then the reinsurers in the first tier, is also reduced. So now we have three tiers of coverage (primary insurance and two layers of excess of loss reinsurance) spread around twenty-five insurers. The twenty reinsurers in the third tier may in turn retain a portion of the risk and then reinsure to a fourth tier of reinsurers and then a fifth tier, and so on and so forth. Through the simplicity of excess of loss reinsurance, the risk of catastrophe is sliced up, parceled out and diversified, with the reinsurers in the highest tier taking the smallest portion of premium as the probability of loss ever reaching their levels is remote, relative to the insurers in the tiers below them.

We can see that the structure which excess of loss reinsurance builds is like an inverse pyramid, with the original risks acquired by the insurer through the homeowners' policies it issues, being parceled out in tiers, with each tier retaining some risk and then passing the remaining risk to the next tier which contains even more reinsurers. Whilst the reinsurers in the very top tier bear the ultimate risk of catastrophe when the size of the losses are such as to exhaust all tiers below them, not only is the probability of this ever happening remote (meaning these reinsurers can build up the premium over many years to pay for such eventuality), but when a catastrophic event does happen there are enough of them in the top tier to ensure the risk has been spread around.

This, then, is how excess of loss reinsurance works and Lloyd's pioneered it. Lloyd's in itself is not a single insurer, but a collection of insurers known as underwriting syndicates all of which are backed by their own capital base. Each syndicate sits in the Lloyd's building on Lime Street in the City of London where they trade under the Lloyd's brand. More often than not the syndicates trade among themselves. Hence, in an excess of loss reinsurance structure, you commonly see several Lloyd's syndicates sitting in each tier and then passing the risk on to other Lloyd's syndicates in the upper tiers. This is partly how Lloyd's has been at the forefront of insurance innovation, as new iterations of insurance can be discussed by the entire market and standards agreed so it can quickly take hold.

We saw this with the development of excess of loss reinsurance. Primarily, in the first half of the twentieth century, excess of loss reinsurance was only used to parcel out a particular large risk, say an oil rig, across the entire Lloyd's market. However, following the devastating losses of Hurricane Betsy in 1965, Lloyd's soon developed an excess of loss reinsurance contract which could protect all policies written by an insurer in any given year (known as 'whole account' excess of loss reinsurance). In providing this protection to an insurer, a Lloyd's syndicate might in a single excess of loss reinsurance contract be acquiring exposure to several different types of insurance written by the insurer (homeowners, auto, personal accident, etc.).

Conceptually whole account excess of loss reinsurance works well, as the plethora of different types of insurance adds a further level diversification into the mix. Indeed whole account excess of loss was one of the reasons that for 300 years Lloyd's was able successfully to manage some of the largest risks the world has ever known, thereby providing the foundation for development and innovation across society.

In the late 1980s, however, the excess of loss reinsurance contract hit that moment in the financial innovation cycle, when the combination of very high demand and standardization moved it away from its original achievement of diversification. Here's what happened.

Massive increases in urbanization led to property being concentrated in single areas, which in turn meant that the size of losses, which insurers would face if a catastrophe hit, increased exponentially. This increased levels of demand for insurance and for whole account excess of loss reinsurance to absorb those heightened levels of risk. In short, through whole account reinsurance, more tiers of reinsurers were added on to ensure greater risk spread. To cope with this demand, however, Lloyd's syndicates needed more and more capital and so went on recruitment drives for investors, lowering their eligibility standards from significantly wealthy rich individuals, to members of the middle class who through rising property prices used their homes as collateral to show they met the minimum asset qualifications. Profits swelled and all seemed good.

Below the veneer, however, disaster was building. The idea of the whole account reinsurance was for a Lloyd's syndicate in an upper tier to take on the risk of the entire portfolio of risks written by the Lloyd's syndicate in the lower tier. Every time risk was passed on to an upper tier, the risk would reduce (as the more tiers there were below a reinsurer, the more capacity there was that had to be exhausted, before the reinsurer at the top had to pay out).

However, with the increasing levels of tiers, it became harder to see exactly what risk Lloyd's syndicates in the higher tiers were taking on.

For example, Lloyd's syndicate A might sit in Tier 1 and then reinsure its whole account (less its retention) to Tier 2, in which Lloyd's Syndicate B sits. Lloyd's Syndicate B would in turn reinsure its whole account (less its retention) to Tier 3, in which Lloyd's Syndicate C sits, which in turn would retain some risk and reinsure its whole account to Lloyd's Syndicate D in Tier 4. Lloyd's Syndicate D might then look for a Tier 5 to pass on its excess risk. Guess who sits in Tier 5? Lloyd's Syndicates A and B – the same reinsurers who sit in Tiers 1 and 2.

Given the number of Tiers below them, however, Lloyd's Syndicates A and B would not appreciate that they had already written the same risk in Tier 5, as they had in Tiers 1 and 2. When their accounts are exhausted in Tiers 1 and 2 therefore, they would remain exhausted should the losses ever hit Tier 5, hence the risk would be passed straight onto the reinsurers in Tier 6 at that stage. Put simply, this incestuous pass-the-parcel, meant certain Tiers in the structure were becoming phantoms, leading to higher probability of reinsurers in the higher Tiers getting hit, than had originally been appreciated.

This problem was compounded by the fact that the increasing number of Tiers had led reinsurers in the upper Tiers to believe that the probability of them ever getting hit was so remote that they could take on more risk in these Tiers. As a result, the inverse pyramid structure, which excess-of-loss reinsurance originally aimed to create, eventually became diamond-shaped, as the very top tiers were placed with fewer and fewer Lloyd's syndicates, comfortable with what they thought was a lower probability of getting hit as a result of being so high up in the structure.

Put simply, the failure to innovate beyond the whole account excess of loss re-insurance, meant that it ended up doing precisely the opposite of what it had aimed to avoid.

Instead of diversifying risk to the many, it had concentrated it on the few. Further, the few on whom the risk had been concentrated were the new middle-class investors, or Names as they are called, whom Lloyd's had specifically gone out to recruit, to cope with increased demand.

When a series of catastrophes hit in the 1980s, the pass-the-parcel spiral which the Lloyd's Market had created, began to unwind and a large section of its Names faced absolute financial ruin. Becoming a Name in a Lloyd's syndicate back then was like becoming a shareholder in a company, save in one crucial respect. A shareholder's liability is limited to the amount of its shareholding i.e. the shareholder cannot lose more than the amount for which he purchased the shares. Lloyd's Names, by contrast, faced unlimited liability, meaning they paid until all losses had been paid; not even bankruptcy could save them from this eventuality. For some, years of savings disappeared in an instant. For others, suicide appeared their only option.

Levelling up the generations
The problems Lloyd's of London went through in the 1980s demonstrate the effects of how holding onto a financial innovation to the point where it ceases to address the problem it originally solved, can be dangerous. They also show us how experience – in this case three hundred years of experience – can, at best, count for absolutely nothing and, at worst, have the power to destroy. Many of the new Names enticed to invest their money at Lloyd's in the 1980s paid the ultimate price for doing so. Why did they invest? – Because of the three hundred years of insurance experience Lloyd's looked back on and wore as a badge of honour.

Lloyd's of London, however, still stands today, its reputation having recovered almost to the point where it once was before the crisis that beset it. This it achieved because it went back to its innovative roots, reinventing itself with one of the most audacious business plans ever to have been implemented in the City of London.[61] The survival of Lloyd's, therefore, stands not only as a testament to the insurance industry's ability to adapt, but shows how there is a need for even those institutions with the most historic roots continually to learn new things and youthful methods of working.

Instead of relating the story of Lloyd's reinvention, however, I have a more personal tale to tell, one which emerged from the Lloyd's crisis and demonstrates how reverse mentoring can lead to reinvention and survival at a very human level. It is a tale which tells how reverse mentoring actually helped save my family.

My father, Anthony John Gregoire, spent his career as a marine insurance broker working in Hong Kong, Greece and then the City of London, all for a single employer. He was very much the last of a generation which believed that staying with the same company throughout one's career was the right thing to do.

I had a wonderful childhood with two loving parents, who guided me morally, made me see the value of hard work, and supported me without spoiling me. If there was a definition for what counted as middle class, my family ticked every box. Financially, the income of both my parents made us comfortable without being rich. Our story, perhaps, is boring in this respect, but wonderfully so.

Like many members of the middle class, my father became a Lloyd's Name as part of its 1980s recruitment drive. He did not quite satisfy the minimum financial eligibility criteria, but his company put up a guarantee for him to join as a reward for his thirty years of loyal service. This happened in 1988, the first year in which Lloyd's made a loss in its three hundred year history. This was followed by further losses in 1989 and 1990, at which point my father called it quits and resigned his investment. However, the three years he was a Name remained open until all losses were paid, which meant my father remained liable. That was the deal.

The Lloyd's syndicates which my father's investment backed called in the guarantee his employer had made. His employer, in turn, looked to my father for reimbursement. Dad refused to pay, not because he didn't want to, but because the well was dry. His savings had already been used to pay all the massive cash calls Lloyd's had so far made. All we had left was the house, which had been sensibly transferred into my mother's name and couldn't be touched, or so we thought.

This was a time of consolidation in the insurance industry. Cost cuts and expense savings were the fashion for management back then (much as they are today) and my father paid the ultimate price. Not long after his fiftieth birthday, he was made redundant, thirty years of experience and loyalty counting for little in the eyes of the overpaid management consultants advising his employer. To add insult to injury the new management sought to offset the amount my father still owed them for paying Lloyd's under the guarantee, from his redundancy payment. It was cruel, but it was business.

This happened in 1997, the year in which I graduated from law school. I remember getting the call from Dad with the news that he had lost his job. He had withheld this from me, until after my final exams so I didn't get distracted. I told him off for that, there was no way he and Mum should have borne this on their own. But that was my Mum and Dad for you, putting my interests first as always.

That summer turned out to be one of the most intense periods for our family. Mum continued to work, so I was at home with Dad for around six weeks before I was due to move to London to start work as a trainee solicitor. The days were beautifully hot, one of the finest summers in years, and a lot was going on the world. Hong Kong was handed back to China. Princess Diana tragically died in a car accident in Paris. For me, however, I will always remember those weeks as the moment my father descended into his own personal hell and then rose from the ashes.

Dad started off the summer by looking for a new job in the insurance industry. Insurance was, after all, all he knew. But it had been over thirty years since he had looked for a job, so even writing his CV was a challenge. Rejection after rejection mounted. Friends said they would let him know of any opportunities they heard about, which meant there was nothing going now. I remember we used to drive to the Job Centre together, so Dad could sign on for unemployment benefits. It was an experience he hated, even though it was nothing he wasn't owed, having paid into the public pot for years. To Dad, however, it felt like a handout, like he was getting something for nothing. It was humiliation, but he swallowed his pride and did it anyway for his family, like he had always done.

But a man can only take so many setbacks and I could see the cracks beginning to show. Dad was drinking more to drown his sorrows. At first, I understood, but when I began finding vodka bottles hidden round the house and catching him with a glass at nine in the morning, I knew we had a problem.

It was after I had fought a glass out of his hands one morning, when we had both screamed at each other in a way that left us both sobbing and angry, that Dad revealed the full extent of what was happening. Sure, his employers had let him have his redundancy payment in the end. But they still wanted what was owed to them for paying Lloyd's under the guarantee and they had one key lever left at their disposal: they still controlled access to his pension.

So that was it. They were threatening to take away his and my mother's ultimate safety net, unless he paid up. That was their way of trying to get at the house. It was cruel, ruthless and brutal, but it was clever.

In my father's eyes, what his employer was trying to do meant ultimate failure for him. It meant he had stepped onto a train every day for thirty-five years and gone to work for nothing. One mistake, one bad investment had cost us everything, that's how he felt.

We went for lots of walks that summer. I made sure we did, to get him out of the house and away from the booze. We talked like we had never done before and I learned so much about my father, that I had never previously known. This was the moment, perhaps, where he stopped being my father and instead became my best friend, one who confided everything in me. He told me all his weaknesses, all his personal fears growing up and I began to know him as a human being with the same frailties we all have, rather than the father whom I thought invincible. Somehow, knowing what he had been through for us made me love him all the more. It made me understand the true meaning of character, that determination always to do the right thing even though we are weak.

Dad taught me a lot on those walks. Here I was, about to start my career in London at the end of the summer, getting a bird's eye view of it from a man who had been there most of his career. He taught me how cruel a place the world I was about to step into could actually be. The politics; the bosses that would smile to your face and stab you in the back after stealing your ideas; the stress of it all. There were also many good times, however, the strong bonds of friendships he had formed with colleagues across the insurance industry, the work they had done in the trenches together.

Amazingly, despite all it had done to him, my father still venerated the insurance industry. He taught me how insurance managed risk, how it had done so since the days of the Babylonian merchants. In the same way those merchants would never have ventured out onto the seas to trade in strange lands, so today satellites wouldn't be launched into space, or massive skyscrapers built and societies developed, unless there was insurance in place enabling it all to happen. No one would put their capital at risk without insurance. Insurance is the engine of human progress. It was that simple. No matter that the industry he worked for had chewed him up and spat him out, Dad still believed in its value, and during those walks, he passed that lesson onto me.

There was something so strangely fragile and yet wonderful about those walks. I was getting to know my father in a different way for the first time. We became equals, where once he had been my superior. We became friends, where once we had been father and son. But it felt like time was ticking away. In September, I would be relocating to London, and with Mum still working, Dad would be left on his own all day at home. If that happened, he would destroy himself, I could see that now and I vowed not to let that happen.

So I began to do things which I had never done before. I took away all the letters from the debt collectors and told Dad he was never to look at them again. From now on, I would take care of those. He protested at first, but I told him that since he had paid for my education, he might as well be the first beneficiary of it!

I also began to teach him a thing or two. Dad may not have known the first thing about job-hunting, but I was from a generation that was expert in the process. Jobs were scarce for graduates in those days, as they are now. Looking for an opportunity was a full time occupation and it had been my obsession during my final year at university. My sole aim had been to find a law firm willing to give me a training contract and I had to compete with thousands of others doing the same. My grades were good, but so were everybody else's, so it was all about showing firms what extra I could bring, demonstrating that I was worth the bet. It was these extras which the interviewers always concentrated on. They liked that I had captained my cross-country team because that showed leadership, independence and determination. They liked that I had spent summers working as a kitchen porter in a factory canteen because it showed an ability to adapt to anything.

I passed on these lessons to Dad. Don't step straight back into the insurance world, I told him. He needed a period to de-clutter his mind from all of that, instead of brooding on it. He needed to try something totally new that would broaden his experience, if only for a few months. It would give him some sense of routine back, and perhaps the opportunity to use his experience in a different way.

The year I had spent job-hunting myself meant that scanning the classifieds was still a habit. I noted that the taxi company just up the road from us was looking for drivers. When I showed it to Mum, we both knew it made sense. Dad loved driving and somehow we could both picture him doing that. The truth was that neither of us wanted him to return to London or insurance. It had become a hell for him and he deserved to spend the rest of his life away from it.

So we set about convincing him. Not in a way which was "in your face", but on those walks I would turn the subject onto the driving holidays we had been on in years gone by and reminisced about how Dad had taught me to drive. Soon we eased onto the subject of driving as a career opportunity. We talked about driving-instructing and long-distance lorry-driving, but then it was Dad himself who brought up the idea of being a taxi-driver, by mentioning that a London cabbie had once won the TV quiz show, "Mastermind". The man's brain had been amazingly well-developed from learning "the Knowledge", as the mastery of London's street-names, buildings, locations, and transport system, required of all London taxi-drivers, is known. "Must be nice meeting all those new people, and driving around all day knowing exactly where to go," Dad commented.

I had the newspaper with the advert ready when we got home. Mum weighed in as planned, telling him what a great idea she thought it was. Why didn't he just ring the number? He could try it just for a few months as a hobby. Think of the stories he could tell.

So Dad picked up the phone. He was nervous, I could see that, but he took the first step to a new career which lasted until the end of his life.

Dad turned being a taxi-driver into a mix of student, psychiatrist and confessional priest. Where before he had never talked about his work, now he couldn't wait to get home and tell us about his day. He felt part of the community's rich social fabric, driving around people from all walks of life. From famous conductors, to ex-Prime Ministers, to single-mothers (who gave him their babies to hold whilst they got their money out to pay), to ex-convicts he'd pick up from court – he drove them all. Insurance, he had once told me, was a people business and that was what he loved about it. But when he became a taxi-driver, it seemed his previous thirty-five years of experience had been just a preparation for a career which now gave him access to all different kinds of people. The old ladies he used to take down to the shops loved his attitude, welcoming smile and the chance to chat. I remember being at home one day, when one of his regulars phoned up, an old man called Dicky. Since Dad wasn't home, Dicky took it upon himself to tell me all about his life story, including how he had once been prosecuted for shooting an intruder with an air-gun! But, most of all, Dicky said how good a man my Dad was because he listened, spoke to him on the same level (when no one else did) and never talked down to him.

The summer of 1997, then, was a turning point for my father. He had fallen, but then risen to heights he had never felt possible, in finding his true vocation and place at the heart of the community. All of this because of those summer walks we went on, when our relationship changed to one of equality and the mix of our combined experience led to both our lives changing. That is the true power of reverse mentoring, two generations bringing their combined experience together to solve real-life problems.

When I left home in September 1997, I knew Mum and Dad would be all right. Because of what we had been through that summer, I had a full appreciation of the sacrifices they had both made for me. There were no better parents I could wish for in this world.

Yet it was still with trepidation that I started work in the City, knowing what it had done to Dad. Reconciling the cruel ruthlessness of the place with the values Mum and Dad had taught me was something that I knew I would find difficult. It would be a struggle, but it was a struggle for which I felt ready.

As for those debt-collectors from Dad's old company, they came hard at me, still demanding their money. In my first meeting with them, they even suggested my parents increase the mortgage on their home to pay. I told them to go to hell with that idea. But I gave them an alternative. If they brought the sum down, I would pay it myself, even though I owed them nothing and, at the start of my career, had nothing.

They rejected this offer at first, so I re-presented it. It went up a level of management and was rejected again.

Then something amazing happened. It reached the General Counsel of the company and in a letter I shall never forget, he wrote to me declaring that the debt was being written off altogether. It was a letter which ended my family's hell, but it also taught me that in the quagmire of ruthlessness that was the City of London, pockets of decency still existed.

Yes, it took a General Counsel – a lawyer working in an insurance company – to put decency ahead of the law.

And in that moment, I knew what career I wanted to pursue.

PART III

CLOSING ARGUMENTS

Chapter 12

THE BENEFITS OF REVERSE MENTORING

So let's recap.

Reverse mentoring is the process by which a younger person mentors an older person, introducing the older person to new concepts and showing him what today's world looks like through youthful eyes. The older person benefits from a refreshing new outlook, which, when combined with his experience, produces a reinvigorated but practical creativity. The younger mentor also benefits, through the opportunity to test his ideas against the reality-check of his older protégé's experience, gaining priceless feedback on how to bring cutting-edge ideas to fruition.

That is the key point of reverse mentoring. It is a bilateral not a binary relationship. The learning flows both ways to create a result far greater than the sum of its parts. Two generations combine youthful imagination and real-life experience, and come away with something very much better than either one would have done on their own. Further, it sends a message that young people are not just about the future, they are about the present too and have an equal responsibility in the problem-solving which needs to be done today.

I first discovered reverse mentoring through the influence of my eight-year-old cousin, a rambunctious know-it-all half-Korean kid called Anthony. Fate threw us together in a relationship of equality even though we were thirty years apart in age. Anthony felt he could say anything to me without my judging him. I felt I could talk with him on the same level, not as a superior. This opened a whole new world up to me, the world Anthony inhabited. Perhaps it was a world I had visited before when I was

Anthony's age, but here I was viewing it again through his young eyes, only this time with the benefit of my thirty-plus years of experience. It had a profound impact on me, altering my perception and shaking me out of the settled, falsely self-satisfied state into which I had lapsed.

My gut told me there was no way I could have been the first person in the world to have benefited from "reverse mentoring" Something this powerful had to have come from deeper roots than the "pop" version which was doing the rounds in the corporate world, where its claim to fame was teaching old guys how to use social media. Turns out, my gut instinct was right.

The roots of reverse mentoring stretch way back. Some of the best-of-the-best on our planet have been its beneficiary. It has been responsible for some extraordinary accomplishments, major societal movements and progressive innovations. Its absence can also account for some of the destruction reaped through the over-reliance placed on past experience.

The evidence of just some of the major benefits of reverse mentoring has been laid out in the pages of this book. From this, we can distil its impact into the following five key positive impacts.

1. Reverse mentoring re-engages the child-like mind

As children our minds are naturally explorative. We have no limits, no pre-conception of danger or risk, no pre-existing notions as to what combination of things works best, or not at all. Because of this, we are eager to learn everything and experiment with anything. We are a blank sheet of paper, happy to scrawl whatever we like, going outside the lines and even outside the page. We don't care if crayons, cornflakes and glue aren't the most natural of bedfellows. We're going to mix them together anyway, just to see what the result is. All of this exploration has a name. It's called playing.

During our playful exploration, however, we eventually find where the limits lie and begin to bind ourselves up in them. At some point the playing stops, we adopt adult ways and conform to social norms. We develop opinions and experience from which we learn lessons for the future. We begin to be rewarded for this growing experience. People give us recognition, we develop self-esteem and this drives us onwards to develop our experience even more.

All of this is as it should be. It's called growing up. It's the learning process in action. Yet, it comes with a significant downside. As we get older and our opinions and experience deepen, our minds tighten. The experience we once venerated now confines us within its limits. When faced with anything different, we instinctively retreat into what we know. The very experience which brought us to the heights of achievement prevents us from further progression. Our experience makes us adopt a veneer of arrogance to protect ourselves against any challenges. Worse, it can trigger a downward spiral that may eventually condemn us to the depths of despair.

It is at this point reverse mentoring is needed. It is at this moment that reverse mentoring can break us free from our constraints with the liberating re-discovery of the child-like playfulness we once had.

It happened to Napoleon. At the hour of his darkest moment, when he had fallen from the greatest of imperial heights into humiliating exile on St Helena, an island quite literally in the middle of no-where, that was the moment Napoleon met fourteen-year-old Betsy Balcombe. The British public laughed as reports of his puerile antics with Betsy hit the tabloids. But the last laugh was to be Napoleon's precisely because of Betsy. Her youthful influence not only broke Napoleon out of the depths of depression, it inspired him to throw his energy into the project of recording the remarkable tale of his life. The raw material was already there because of Napoleon's achievements, but it was a story that needed passion and energy to tell and this is exactly what Napoleon threw into the task of having his memoirs recorded by Las Casas, the last great project of the former emperor's life. Napoleon's memoirs, published after his death, became an instant bestseller and one of the most-read books of the 19th century. Betsy had rejuvenated Napoleon's mind to enable him to create his legacy. It is because of this that every school student knows his name today.

Centuries later, when my cousin Anthony forced me to get on a bus with him without knowing the destination and we started making up ridiculous stories about the people we saw down on the pavements, I felt my own child-like mind being rekindled. Anthony's influence changed my outlook. He, quite literally, rejuvenated me.

Reconnection to the child-like mind gives a person with experience the freshest of perspectives when he or she needs it the most. It is a shot of adrenalin, a wake-up call, pure reinvigoration. It gives us back that restlessness we once had, when we were young and in a hurry and eager to make things happen. It makes the whole merry-go-round of life seem fun again.

But let's not forget that reverse mentoring is a two-way street. The young mentors also walk away with something too. In return for re-introducing their older protégés to their own imagination, the younger mentors gain a new playmate and a friendship which is entirely different from anything they have had before. Betsy Balcombe would never have played with her parents the way she did with Napoleon. She found herself probably the only person in the world able to ask Napoleon openly about the most controversial aspects of his career. No one else would have dared. Betsy learned a valuable life skill here: how to connect with people of any background, for if she could connect with Napoleon on an equal level, there were no limits she could not pass over.

2.   Reverse mentoring creates "controlled imagination"

"Controlled imagination" was a phrase first coined by the Field Marshall Viscount Slim KG, GCB, GCMC, GCVO, GBE, DSO, MC, KStJ.62 Impressive though his lengthy title is, Bill Slim was probably the most down-to-earth general the British army has ever known. Unlike his Second World War counterpart, Field Marshall Montgomery, who craved publicity and the limelight, Slim positively shied away from it. That's probably why everyone knows Montgomery's name, but Slim's remains one hardly recognised by the general public.

Bill Slim was given command of the First Burma Corps in the South-East Asian theatre during the Second World War in 1942 at a time when things were, to put it mildly, going badly for the Allies. The British Army was in full retreat in Burma, in the face of the advancing Japanese forces. Slim's immediate task was to ensure that the retreat was as successful as it could be, by saving every man he could so they would live to fight another day. The Burma retreat turned out to be a miraculous effort of endurance. Although many men were lost in the awful conditions they faced, the retreat was every bit as successful as the Dunkirk evacuation had been, a testament to Slim's extraordinary leadership. Often he was at the coal-face, urging his men on, talking with them one-to-one, keeping the momentum going.

Yet, unlike Dunkirk, the Burma retreat went without any accolades back in Britain. Rather, it was deemed a humiliation, with Winston Churchill himself venting his disappointment at the army's performance. Once the retreat was complete, Slim – refusing to accept this negative evaluation of his men – determined to turn defeat into victory. He accomplished this, using his concept of "controlled imagination". By "imagination", he meant creative re-thinking of the army's strategy and tactics. As for "control", this came from his experience of years of soldiering, ensuring his new ideas led to a strategy that could be implemented in reality.

During the retreat, the myth had built up amongst the British forces, that the fanaticism of the Japanese made them super-soldiers and invincible. Slim imaginatively decided to use this trait against his enemy, in what he called his "hammer and anvil" strategy.[63] Central to this was the formation of his forces into strongholds called "administrative boxes". These strongholds would serve as the "anvil" and would hold their positions with 360 degree defensive perimeters, drawing wave after wave of Japanese attack. The attacks would be predictable, precisely because of the Japanese army's fanaticism, and they would intensify as the Japanese supply chains became exhausted, making continued advance the enemy's only option. At that point the trap would be set and the hammer would be deployed in the form of relieving British forces, attacking from the flank or rear to crush the Japanese against the anvil of the box.

Slim was able to couple this imaginative strategy with the experience which gave him an understanding of what was needed to make it a success. This was controlled imagination at its best, where creative strategic thinking was made real by applying experience to get things done.

First, Slim realized that the stronghold "box" would need to be continuously supplied with munitions and supplies from the air in order to be able to hold out. He instructed his officers to instill "air-mindedness" amongst the men, so they could understand that a supply chain from the air was as effective as one on the ground. They were not, in short, cut-off, just because the supplies could not make it over land. Secondly, he organized war-games and intensive jungle-training for the men, instilling within them the notion that the jungle was as much a friend to them in warfare as it was to the Japanese.

In 1944, the Japanese launched Operation Ha-Go at the British forces in the Arakan. Ha-Go (which translates as "headlong attack") was the exact tactic that Slim had been preparing his army to counter. The Japanese expected the British forces to yield in ten days, but the administrative boxes held firm. Further intensive fighting cut off the British land supply routes, but Slim counteracted the effect sof this by the air supplies he had planned for. Everything was resupplied to the "box" within forty-eight hours of its running out. In the meantime, the hammer of the 26th Division made steady progress. After almost three weeks of continuous fighting, the Japanese – their supplies dwindling – were forced to retreat; and were pursued by the "hammer" of the British forces, thus well and truly shattering the myth of Japanese invincibility.

This was the turning point, but fierce fighting still lay ahead of the British forces under Slim's command, as the Japanese launched another campaign to infiltrate India. Again the administrative boxes held firm in the defences of Kohima and Imphal. At Imphal in particular, Slim saw his strategy coming to fruition as the Japanese virtually destroyed themselves with suicidal bitter attacks which annihilated their fighting capabilities. This set the stage for the re-entry and recapture of Burma by Slim and his 14th Army, which he accomplished in 1945. This was something which had seemed impossible three years earlier, but, with the deployment of controlled imagination, became reality, earning Slim the deserved accolade of being one of Britain's greatest ever generals.

Slim's notion of "controlled imagination" is essentially a combination of creative ideas backed up by the operational experience needed to turn the ideas into reality. It is exactly this combination which reverse mentoring creates.

Today, with constant access to technology and communication across the world, a generation has grown up which is incredibly adept at "raising awareness" about particular issues. Indeed "raising awareness" for a condition or a plight has become a goal in its own right, charities and other not-for-profit organisations being set up with this precise goal in mind. Noble though "raising awareness" is, however, it should only ever be seen as a job half-done. There is little point in having awareness of a problem unless an attempt is made to try to solve or ameliorate it. This is where the "raising awareness" generation falls short, precisely because they lack practical problem-solving experience. Members of the older generation, however, have spent their careers encountering and solving problems. So much so, in fact, that their imaginations have likely become blunted by cynicism.

Both generations have their strengths and both have their weaknesses. Throw them together in a relationship of reverse mentoring and the strengths balance out the weaknesses. The imagination of the younger generation combines with the experience of the older generation to produce controlled imagination.

Problem, quite literally, solved

3. Reverse mentoring pushes knowledge and experience beyond its boundaries

Reverse mentoring creates conditions which push both participants beyond their limits. Take Winston Churchill as an example. He had ridden in the British army's last cavalry charge. He had escaped from prison in the Boer war. He had held all the great offices of state and seen action in the trenches of World War I. He had been cast out as a reactionary warmonger, only to be brought back into power again when his country's existence was facing the gravest threat in its history. He was a man of vast experience, who had seen it and done it all and his speeches had served to lift a nation's morale at its darkest hour during the summer of 1940.

Yet even a man like Churchill found in the inspiration of youth the impulse needed to push his massive experience beyond its limits. In those silent five minutes on the ride back to Chequers with "Pug" Ismay, after witnessing the deployment of young RAF pilots into the Battle of Britain, Churchill utilised the emotion inspired by the selfless sacrifice of these young men, to push beyond his oratorical boundaries. His immense knowledge of the English language was marshalled in that juggernaut mind of his to find the right words to capture the mix of pride, honour, emotion, determination and sheer gratitude that he was feeling, so the British nation could feel the same.

Days later when Prime Minister Churchill told Parliament "never in the field of human conflict, has so much been owed by so many to so few", he pushed the power of oratory to new heights to lift people's souls and spread a deep sense of gratitude and duty across his country, which not only drove Britain on to victory in the Second World War, but changed the character of the nation for future generations.

This is reverse mentoring at its most powerful and it works both ways. Manny Pacquiao had already been turned into a complete fighter by the experienced Freddie Roach. But it was Freddie's continued desire to work up-close with his fighters, toe-to-toe in the ring, which one day, in one of their mitt-work sessions, inspired Manny to try something different, to come at Freddie from an angle. Freddie loved it and together they used Manny's innovative counter-attack to create a new style of boxing, which Manny pioneered, to become one of the greatest fighters of his generation.

4. Reverse mentoring as a mechanism for life-long learning

Reverse mentoring can be part of a lifelong learning process from which both participants benefit. Through reverse mentoring, the learning process becomes less about simple knowledge transfer, and more about the development of our existing knowledge so that it can be applied in a practical away in completely new directions. This is done by throwing the participants together in a relationship which takes them both outside their comfort zone and results in them pushing each other beyond their existing limits.

The young mentors are either still going through, or not long out of, the formal part of their education. At this point their minds are crammed full of knowledge they have learned in a school-type setting. Although they have the knowledge, however, they lack the skills to turn their knowledge into practical use.

The older protégés offer a complete contrast. Often they have forgotten most of what they learned in school or university. This has been subsumed by the practical skill-set they have been exercising every day for decades. So adept are they at exercising these skills, that they have become second nature. In becoming second nature, however, the development of these skills has plateaued. The older protégés have probably lapsed into their own comfort zone, so, in exercising their skills, they are quite literally just going through the motions.

In isolation, each of these traits is a weakness. Knowledge without the ability to apply it is redundant. Practical skills which have plateaued become more out of date with every passing day as the world moves on. In combination, however, these weaknesses morph into compounded strengths.

An example of this happened in 1968 during the Vietnam war. During the first six months of that year US fighter pilots engaged in dog-fights with North-Vietnamese pilots flying Russian-made MiG fighter planes. The results of these air-to-air combat engagements were pretty even, with the same number of planes being shot down by both sides. The US navy resolved to break this stalemate, however, and gain air superiority. To do this they knew they needed to improve their pilots' win ratio. So they set up the US Navy Strike Fighter Tactics Instructor Program, aka 'Top Gun school' to teach young navy pilots how to fight more effectively and increase their success rate.[64]

At Top Gun school, the best and most experienced navy pilots were recruited to train the navy's most talented but newest fighter pilots. Teaching took place not in the classroom, but in the air, through mock air-to-air dogfights between the teachers and the students, each pushing their planes to the limit and trying out new tactics in different situations to see what worked and what didn't. The planes were armed with cameras, so that, after a fight, teacher and student could go over the video, see exactly what happened and work out what could have been done better. After the training, the young pilots would return to their units and put into practice what they had learned.

What was interesting, however, was how the learning went both ways. Whilst the students would return to their units after the course, the teachers stayed on to teach the next class. The teachers therefore accumulated more and more hours of mock dog-fight experience, learning new skills each time, as successive students tested out new tactics, pushing the teachers beyond their limits. In turn, the teachers would pass on their skills to the students, who would improve and keep trying out new things every time they took on their teachers in the air. It became a spiral of continual improvement for both parties and the improvement quickly bore out in the numbers. Between 1970 and 1973, US pilots shot down on average 12.5 North Vietnamese planes for every one US plane which was lost. Superiority in the air was established.

We see in this example the reverse mentoring dynamic at work, both counterparts using their knowledge to push the other to improve beyond their constraints. The younger mentor's improvement comes from getting the practical experience to deploy their talent. The older protégé's improvement comes from having their existing skill-set, pushed constantly beyond their comfort zone.

Indeed, for the older protégé in this scenario, the simple act of teaching becomes a learning experience in itself. It involves the teacher having to examine his skill-set, break it down into different components and then teach the student how to get good at each component before putting the whole thing together. By doing this, the teacher re-learns his skill, but in a way he hasn't done before and this new perspective gives him the opportunity to push beyond the boundaries.

Perhaps the best example of life-long learning comes from the relationship we saw between Supreme Court Justice Oliver Wendell Holmes Jr. and academic Harold Laski in Chapter 6. Laski, at twenty-four years old, was able to invigorate Holmes's powerful judicial mind by suggesting reading material. The result was Holmes's dissenting opinion in *Abrams v United States*, written when Holmes was seventy-eight years old. To this day it provides one of the most powerful, yet simple, defences of free-speech known to the world. The notion of the "free trade in ideas" also provides foundation to the concepts of diversity and inclusion.

5.   Reverse mentoring as a path to fulfilment
Earlier in the book we introduced Maslow's hierarchy of needs and how the highest level of need a person can fulfill is self-actualization, that point in life where a person knows their purpose and is living in fulfillment of their values.

Reverse mentoring is not a panacea for all participants to achieve self-actualization, but I would certainly make the case that it can assist on the path towards it. We saw this in the relationship between Eleanor Roosevelt and Pauli Murray. Roosevelt had, through her own personal crisis, acquired an openness to people from different backgrounds. She pursued personal friendships with people outside the confines of her own privileged upbringing, with the aim of learning and improving her understanding. Through this openness, Eleanor Roosevelt allowed herself to be inspired by Pauli Murray, a young passionate firebrand who had thrown herself into numerous civil rights causes. The influence of Murray – as well as other friends whom

Roosevelt made through her openness – led to Eleanor Roosevelt achieving a status which no other First Lady has achieved. To this day, she is recognized as a beacon for human rights causes across the world, and stands for the power of diversity to improve society.

Similarly, through Eleanor Roosevelt's encouragement, Pauli Murray pursued the path of civil rights through becoming a lawyer, a writer and then a professor. Later on in her life, Murray became the first African-American woman to be ordained as a priest in the Episcopalian church. It was a position which married Murray's passion for civil rights with the pursuit of pastoral care, thereby enabling her to achieve her true life's purpose.

Roosevelt and Murray provide an extreme example of the power of reverse mentoring, but the dynamic can be used by all to pursue one's true purpose. Through reverse mentoring, the older protégé is afforded the time and space for self-reflection in a way they probably have not had for a long time. The influence of the younger mentor forces the older protégé to ask questions of their life, which in turn reconnects them with the sense of purpose they had when they were their younger mentor's age. At the same time, the younger mentor learns how the search for purpose is a key part of life's journey and understands the importance of starting the search as early as possible.

A quest that never ends and is an end in itself

These then are the five key impacts reverse mentoring brings us. They are profound, life changing impacts. Those who have participated in a reverse mentoring relationship don't just come out of it with knowledge of how to use social media. They emerge as better people, having had the opportunity to develop their character.

When I look back on the relationship I had with my cousin Anthony, I remember how discomforting our first few attempts to get to know each other were. I was not a parent and did not really know how to act around children.

To be fair to myself, Anthony was not the easiest child to get along with and would take delight in testing my patience whenever the opportunity arose.

Yet, looking back, that was part of what made the reverse-mentoring relationship work. Unlike a parent, I had no right to claim superiority over Anthony. A sense of feeling well outside my comfort zone forced me into a place of humility where I had no other choice but to "go with the flow". This imbued the relationship with an equality which would have seemed odd to outside observers because of the difference in ages, but it made perfect sense to us. We were able to joke around and challenge each other because of this equality, but whenever a disagreement occurred, we were able to forgive quickly and move on in the way that equals do.

These ingredients - humility, equality, together with an ability to accept challenges and forgive disagreements – are the key to any successful reverse-mentoring relationship. These are the traits which make a person's character and reverse mentoring helps you develop them.

It is easy to list these traits out on paper, but they are much harder to adopt, internalise and develop. At the outset of reverse mentoring it will feel awkward for both parties, but that is all part and parcel of what makes it work. We learn best when we are pushed out of our comfort zone and that sense of awkwardness is a sign that things are going as they should be. After all, it is when mentor and protégé push themselves beyond their limits, that the true magic of reverse mentoring happens. That is how new ideas emerge and how true character is developed.

I began my reverse-mentoring relationship with Anthony with the unstated aim of bringing out the best in him, as would be the case with any traditional mentoring relationship. It ended up with him challenging me to get the best out of myself. That is reverse mentoring in a nutshell and I hope the foregoing pages have served, if nothing else, to inspire you to take the opportunity to have a go yourself.

For when we set out to bring out the best in others, we open ourselves up to the possibility of others bringing out the best in ourselves; and that is a never-ending quest which is always worth pursuing.

Chapter 13

HOW TO SET UP
A REVERSE-MENTORING SCHEME

After my cousin Anthony passed away, I reflected on the impact that our relationship had had on me. Somehow, Anthony had ignited within me a need to get the best out of myself in my chosen profession, in my passion for writing and in every aspect of my life (see Chapter 3). I found that the incredible dynamic which we had unwittingly stumbled upon was already known, and bore the name, "reverse mentoring". The more I learned about the possibilities of what reverse mentoring could achieve, the more I wanted to establish a formal reverse-mentoring scheme, so that others could reap the benefits outlined in the preceding pages.

So that's exactly what I did. The story of how I went about this is the subject of this final chapter.

The purpose here is not to provide a template which can be blindly followed (if reverse mentoring has taught me anything, it is that "one-size-fits-all" solutions are no solution at all). Rather, it is to offer general guidance as to how it might be done in the hope that you feel sufficiently inspired to set up your own reverse-mentoring scheme and make it even better.

So here it is: my guide to setting up a reverse-mentoring scheme.

Making the commitment
It is easy to have an idea. Implementing it is the tough part. The former is something you have whilst you're brushing your teeth. The latter takes passion, time-commitment and grit. To make your idea reality, you have to commit yourself wholeheartedly to it. Others on the team can help

you, sure, but if you are the first person to put up your hand (and I hope you are) then you have to be the driving force.

I remember the moment I made the commitment. The idea for a reverse-mentoring scheme had been playing at the edges of my mind ever since Anthony passed away, but it was only when, one day, I saw an e-mail from our Head of Human Resources, that the flame inside me was sparked. It called for volunteers to set up Employee Resources Groups (ERGs) within the company to further the "diversity agenda".

Now, I am a cynical sod by nature (most members of the legal profession tend to be). E-mails from Human Resources about their latest waffly new initiative find their way into my "trash" folder faster than Usain Bolt on a gold medal charge! For some reason, however, this one caught my eye long enough to register an interest and trigger a train of thought which ended with the conclusion that this was exactly the vehicle I needed to launch a reverse-mentoring scheme.

So I put up my hand to establish the new Young Talent ERG. As soon as I volunteered, I knew I had to commit one hundred percent. I knew how easily this new ERG could lapse into the usual kind of talking-shop that is the destiny of many HR initiatives, where image takes precedence over substance. I was absolutely determined to ensure that the Young Talent ERG would not suffer this fate. So I made a pledge with myself. From that moment on, I was fully committed to make it work and to achieve something meaningful. Image could go to hell. Substance would reign.

With hindsight, I can tell you that an ERG is a perfect vehicle for establishing a reverse-mentoring scheme. Because of the kind of people it attracts to volunteer, an ERG serves the purpose of embedding a rich diversity into any corporate culture (and yes, I have become less cynical because I have witnessed this). So if you are looking to set up a scheme within a business organization, consider establishing an ERG. It is not the only available vehicle, of course. Your company or indeed your school, university, club or organization may already have an existing social or welfare committee which you can use. If not, just set one up.

But when you do, do yourself a favour. Commit wholeheartedly, make the pledge to be "all in" from the outset, because a reverse-mentoring scheme is not a short-term initiative. It is a long-term experience which needs sustained commitment to succeed.

Putting together your core team
You cannot do it on your own. You need a core team of equally committed people to help you. These are the worker bees, the people who have to book venues, send out e-mails, design flyers, help with budgets and scheduling sessions.

I did not have too much difficulty finding people to join the team, once I explained the reverse-mentoring initiative and asked for volunteers. They understood what the reverse-mentoring scheme was aiming for right from the get-go. They liked the fact that it was different and they bought into the vision of making it a substantive initiative that would have an impact at the individual level, rather than being just a cosmetic tick-box achievement.

The reason for volunteering may differ from person to person, but the fact they volunteer at all engenders a commitment in itself and is indicative of the passion you will need to make the scheme work. Do not go out looking for people with particular skill-sets. Passion beats skill every time when setting up a reverse mentoring scheme. Get your volunteers on board first, find out their skills and the type of personalities they are and then design the programme using their skills and, more importantly, their input. Your team's input is vital in this respect. This will make it into their reverse mentoring initiative and when your team takes ownership, the battle is won, because through the long journey ahead you will have people who can be relied on to support each other to reach the destination of success.

Designing your programme

In designing your reverse-mentoring programme, you have to strike the balance between structure and flexibility. The framework should have sufficient structure so your mentors know exactly what they need to do and when they need to do it by. Within that framework, however, you need to give the mentors the freedom to get to know each other, discuss issues, exchange views and build deep and lasting relationships. With this in mind, below is the programme my team designed. It shows you the type of decisions you will have to make.

* **Programme description**

A "Two-Way Mentoring" programme, the purpose of which is to pair up sets of mentors from different generations to mentor each other over a nine-month period.

* **Programme aims**

The programme pairs up members of staff from Generation X (born before 1980) with members of staff from Generation Y (born after 1980) to mentor each other. Each pair of mentors is assigned general discussion topics to stimulate discussion and ideas. The seasoned Generation X mentors will have the opportunity to pass on their advice and experience to their Generation Y counterparts. The Generation Y mentors will in turn obtain, in their Gen X mentors, a sounding board for their own ideas and aspirations. By being exposed to the challenge of new ideas and fresh perspectives, the Generation X mentors will gain the opportunity to put their experience to new-found uses and thereby push beyond their limits. Both participants will come away better for the experience, having had the chance for substantive self-reflection.

* How does the programme work?

The formal part of the programme lasts for nine months, split into three periods of three months each. Each three-month period begins and ends with a plenary session to which all mentors are invited. At the first plenary session, the mentors are formally paired up (this is done randomly), given a short introduction to mentoring, and assigned a discussion topic. During the three months immediately following this (the first three month period), the mentors have to arrange one-on-one meetings in their pairs to discuss the assigned topic and share ideas. At the end of the first three-month period, another all-mentor plenary session is hosted at which the mentor pairings are invited to share what they have learned on the topic during their one-on-one mentor meetings. They are also assigned a second discussion topic, to go away and talk about during the second three-month period, which ends with another all-mentor plenary session, and topic assignment for the final three-month period.

* How does the programme end?

At the end of the nine months, all participating mentors are given the opportunity to join a second mentor programme, in which they can mentor secondary-school pupils. They are also encouraged to continue their mentoring relationships with their existing mentors, and discussion topics can be assigned for this. They can also participate in the next two-way mentoring programme, in which they will have the opportunity to be paired with a different mentor.

*

Recruiting the mentors

Okay, so you have decided to set up your programme, and have set out the framework for how it will be structured. The next challenge you face is how to attract mentors to join the programme.

At the outset of our programme, we had absolutely no idea what the response rate would be. The organizing team did, however, have very defined ideas of the type of people we wanted to target as mentors, particularly from the Generation X population within the company.

Like most businesses, our company already had plenty of HR initiatives targeted at top-performers, high-potential individuals, persons being groomed for leadership roles in the future, and new joiners. However, within any business, in addition to these stand-out personnel, you will find a section of people who have been with the company for some time, doing the same role, who do not stand out.

These people know their craft inside out. They are the doers, the functionaries who understand the "nuts and bolts", and get stuff done. Many of them do not particularly aspire to promotion because they are both comfortable where they are and find satisfaction in what they do. They get on with their job without any fanfare, and because of this, they are easily taken for granted. Make no mistake, however: if this section of staff disappeared, the business would cease to function because they form its back-bone.

It was this section of staff – the people who really make the company work – whom we were targeting for our reverse-mentoring scheme. We recognized that getting them to volunteer would be challenging, precisely because of their type of personality: people who just got things done without raising their heads above the parapets.

So how did we do it? Well, it all started with a simple cup of coffee.

We sat down with the HR department and made a list of the people whom we specifically wanted to volunteer as mentors and then we invited them all out for coffee without telling them why. The lack of reason prompted enough curiosity for our invitation to be accepted.

When they arrived, I told them they were part of a focus group session on a new initiative which The Young Talent ERG was launching, called "two-way mentoring". I set out the high-level principles of what it entailed and said I needed their input on how to design the programme, so as to make it meaningful. I wanted their feedback on the idea and I also wanted their suggestions as to how to make the idea work.

Why them? Because of their experience; because by being invited to this focus group, I was recognizing them as the people who knew how to make things work in this company and that was precisely the kind of advice I needed.

After that, I opened it up for comments. As we went round the table, I was faced with a barrage of exactly what you would expect from staff who have been at a company for such a long time. That special blend of cynicism, world-weariness and understated passion that comes from people who turn up every day to do what needs to be done.

The clear message was, that, to make it meaningful, the programme needed to be different from all the other standard HR initiatives which had become so frequent that people were immune to their impact (this was music to my ears). So what sort of things could we do, to make it meaningful? I asked. The ideas really started to flow.

* Make sure you pair up people from different departments so there's an opportunity to get to know others across the company.
* Don't limit the discussion topics to just work issues.
* Make sure people aren't forced to share everything they discuss with their mentors in the plenary sessions otherwise they may hold back.
* Don't make it too structured.

This feedback was, in essence, flesh being put on the bare bones of the design we had sketched out. Without them realizing it, the people we were targeting as mentors were completing the design of a mentoring programme which they wanted to see. In so doing, they were subconsciously buying in.

Then came my next question: "Do you think people will volunteer?"

Sure, if we took on board their feedback, was the answer.

"That's great," I said before unleashing my final parting shot. "By the way, this is an entirely voluntary programme. But do you know who I think would make the best mentors? You guys. That's why I'm here asking for your advice. You guys know how to make things work. You do it every day and I think the next generation could benefit from your advice, just like I'm benefiting from it now. You said the programme had to be meaningful to work. Well, you are the people who can make it meaningful! The e-mail asking for volunteers goes round next week. I would love it, if I saw some of your names on the response."

I got up and left.

The next week when we sent the e-mail asking for volunteers, we got a hundred percent response rate from those who had participated in the focus group. They had bought in and were in for the long haul. Job done!

Reading this, you may think there was manipulation at play. Well, to that accusation I plead guilty. But I meant every word of what I told these guys. I believed they would be perfect for reverse-mentoring programme. And you know what? I was right.

So that was Generation X taken care of. Getting Generation Y volunteers wasn't too much of a problem. Youth comes untainted with the cynicism of age and open minds lead to curiosity whenever something new is on offer. On the odd occasion when I felt a nudge was needed, I nudged. My refrain of, "Hey, I think you'd be a great reverse mentor", usually did the trick. Susceptibility to flattery is a human failing, but if the means justify the ends, use that failing to your advantage!

One final tip under this section. What's in a name? It turns out, more than we think. If you have reached this stage in the book, you will appreciate that reverse mentoring is a two-way path, where both participants come away with something significant from the process. For many, however, that connotation isn't immediately obvious from the name "reverse mentoring", which suggests that the mentoring is one way, but in the reverse direction. Even at the planning stage, some of my team members bristled at the thought of Generation X staff having to supplicate themselves to mentoring from their Generation Y counterparts. The prospective humiliation, it was felt, would be too much for some people.

They eventually came to accept that reverse mentoring was, in effect, a process of turning traditional mentoring on its head, with counterparts mentoring each other in a relationship of mutuality and equality. But we reached this point only after I had spent some time explaining it. I could have provided this same explanation to all participants in the scheme, perhaps, but that would have left me exhausted. So instead, we decided to tweak the name of the scheme so that it became less allegorical and more literal. Hence, "two-way mentoring" was born.

The point is this: don't be a slave to form. Make whatever tweaks you deem necessary, to ensure your scheme works.

Discussion topics, plenary sessions and momentum

A mentoring scheme is not an overnight fad. It is a long-term process which requires sustained commitment from your mentors. It is important to include, within the scheme framework, elements which keep the momentum going through the full nine months, or however long a period you have selected. Factors to consider here are your choice of discussion-topics and how you run your plenary sessions.

My focus-group feedback had already given me a very clear message, namely to make the reverse-mentoring scheme as different as possible from any of the other standard HR schemes into which staff were being constantly press-ganged. That message became my benchmark for discussion-topic selection and running the plenary sessions.

When choosing the topics, I set out in search of subjects which could, as far as possible, divorce the mentoring process from the work-place, which meant shying away from the usual corporate nonsensical interview questions. I also had in mind the need to give participants time to carry out some much-needed self-reflection. Reverse mentoring, after all, aimed at reinvigorating the Generation X mentors by putting them back in touch with their true purpose in life, as well as allowing Generation Y mentors the opportunity to explore and find their own purpose.

After much deliberation, the discussion topics we selected for each three-month stage of the programme were as follows.

Topic 1	Why do I do what I do?
Topic 2	For Generation X mentors: Based on your experience, what three pieces of advice would you give yourself, if you travelled back in time to meet yourself when you were twenty years old?
	For Generation Y mentors: If you were able to travel forward in time and see yourself when you are fifty years old, what three things would like to see your fifty-year-old self as having accomplished?
Topic 3	Perform a SWOT analysis (i.e. an analysis of Strengths, Weaknesses, Opportunities and Threats) on your mentor counterpart.

Topics 1 and 2 in particular were designed to give the mentors wide scope for self-interpretation and to encourage them to dig deep within themselves to find the answer. We knew they might struggle with these topics, but struggle was good and made easier through discussion with their mentors, who would offer both a sounding board and a fresh perspective on the issue.

For Topic 3 – the SWOT analysis – we did revert to the familiarity of a well-established corporate-style self-help mechanism, but there was method to our madness here. At the end of the mentoring programme, the mentors were going on to mentor secondary-school students and one of the aims of that process would be to help a student conduct a SWOT analysis on him or herself. Hence it was important for our mentors to know how to do it.

We aimed at making the topics cumulative, in the sense that they would allow the mentors not only to reflect on themselves but really to get to know their counterparts, so that the relationship could become more beneficial as time went on. An alternative which we considered for Topic 3 (before going with the SWOT analysis) was, "What three pieces of advice would you give to your fellow mentors and why?" Here we would have seen a natural progression from self-reflection ("Why do I do what I do") to self-advice ("Looking back/ looking forward in time), to advising others ("Three-pieces of advice for your fellow mentors").

Whilst it is hard to generalize, the range of answers which came forth at the plenary sessions demonstrated that the topics certainly hit the mark. Interestingly, the Generation X mentors tended to focus their answers more in the context of work than their Generation Y counterparts. For example, in answering the question, "Why do I do what I do?", Generation X talked about the reason why they came to work every day, whereas Generation Y mentors interpreted it more in line with their endeavours outside of work. The same was true when it came to looking back (for Generation X) and looking forward (for Generation Y) on Topic 2. The diversity of answers, however, certainly made people realize, in Generation X's case, how much work now dominated their existence, and in Generation Y's case, how there was room for work to draw more of their focus.

As for the plenary sessions, it was most important to get the first plenary session right, as this would set the tone for the programme. I was lucky enough to have help from a friend, Thomas Ng, who runs his own business, Practelligence, which focuses on youth work in Hong Kong. The remit I gave him was to make the first plenary session as non-corporate as possible. (Given that he was outside the corporate world, he was a perfect choice for this challenge.) With Thomas's help, our first plenary session was about the most tangential and non-corporate event you can imagine. To introduce mentoring, Thomas demonstrated how (through personal coaching) any one (in this case even a female accountant) can break a board in half with a karate chop! With this, we sent the clear message that this mentor programme was like no other. Provided our mentors showed the same commitment as the lady who had dissected a plank of wood with her bare hands, the benefits would flow.

The remaining plenary sessions did not involve elements as exciting, but the very open spirit of the first session carried on through. These sessions were really for the mentors to share as much as they wanted, about what they had discussed on the topics in their pairs. We made clear that it was entirely voluntary to share and that it was more than okay if there were things they preferred to stay silent on. For each session, to get things rolling, we would pick a pair of mentors and give them advance notice that we wanted them to be the first to speak about what they had discussed. That really was the only pre-work necessary, because after the first pair had spoken, others were more than keen to share their own experience, and we often found ourselves running out of time (a better problem to have, than there being dead air to fill).

Finally, in between sessions, to keep the momentum going, we would send at least one e-mail to the whole group of mentors giving them pointers about how to conduct their discussions, and indicating the results from other mentors who had already discussed the same topics. For this to happen, we had one pair who were ahead in the three-month cycle and who discussed the topics before the other mentors did, so that they could share their results by way of encouragement. (Please see the case study for "Peter and Kanas" in the appendix.)

FINAL NOTE

So there we have it, reverse mentoring in a nutshell and how to set up your own reverse-mentoring scheme. Experience is useless if it is kept under the wraps. Youth is wasted on the young. Mix the two together, however, and you conjure up a cocktail of creativity, as potent as any that exists in this world. That is the power of reverse mentoring.

APPENDIX
Case studies

The following case studies come from the reverse mentoring scheme described in Chapter 13. They provide a powerful illustration of what reverse mentoring can achieve.

Mark and Charmaine

Mark and Charmaine couldn't be more different. Mark, a fifty-five year old casualty underwriter originally from the United Kingdom, by his own admission, "stumbled into" a career in insurance over thirty years ago, quite literally it seems. He was late for his day of work in London, after staying in the pub too long and missing his flight from Jersey the night before. A somewhat unpromising start for someone who has since established himself as a guru of casualty business in Asia.

Mark possesses that cynical sense of humour that comes from making a living evaluating the risk of bodily injury and death. That humour manifests itself every Friday, when Mark pops up in the office in the latest of a seemingly limitless collection of hideously eye-catching, Hippy-esque shirts. For Mark, whilst life is to be taken seriously, its ridiculous elements deserve to be ridiculed and one suspects his choice of shirt on Friday is his way of doing just that.

Charmaine is Mark's polar opposite. A generation Y, fresh-faced, slightly built Hong Kong girl, Charmaine has a constant bright smile, suggestive of someone who sees the world as pure opportunity waiting to be grasped. Beneath this appearance, however, lies the heart and mind of someone keen to contribute to society, coupled with a steely determination which sees this intention converted to reality. A qualified physiotherapist and a doctor of Chinese medicine, Charmaine puts her skills to use helping people overcome workplace injuries as part of an insurance claims team.

Paired together randomly as mentors, Mark and Charmaine immediately found common ground on numerous topics. Charmaine went to university in the United Kingdom, where Mark had worked for a good period of his career. This gave them both different perspectives on many aspects of Hong Kong, Mark as an outsider looking in and Charmaine as an insider but with an international flavour to her outlook. The subject of education in Asia, and the need for it to place significantly more emphasis on critical thought, was one of the many topics they covered in depth during their discussions. Both are also keen long-distance runners and Mark was able to benefit from Charmaine's medical experience to source a decent doctor from his medical insurance provider's panel, who could help him sort out his dodgy knee.

Yet it was when reflecting on the subject of, "Why do I do what I do?", that the reverse-mentoring dynamic took hold and sprouted wings between them. For, in answering this question, Charmaine revealed her mission, to make Chinese medicine available to all, not just through her day job, but for society as a whole.

For a cynic like Mark, such idealism would probably have produced the beginnings of a sympathetic smile at the misguided ambition of youth. But that would have been wiped off his face by Charmaine's next revelation. Charmaine, along with two others, had founded Chinese Medicine for All (CMA), a charity aimed at bringing Chinese medicine to the poorest areas in Asia.

CMA is the Chinese medical equivalent of Medicins Sans Frontier and since its foundation in 2009, it has mounted expeditions to provide medical provision to the Philippines, Myanmar and India. Its mission is not just to treat, but to teach individuals in poor communities how to practice Chinese Medicine, so as to ensure sustainability.

Mark was stunned by this. The Generation Y stereotype is of someone entirely motivated by recognition, who doesn't do anything unless they are seen to be doing it. Yet here was Charmaine, slipping into their conversation this life-defining mission on which she has embarked, almost as an after-thought.

It was at this moment that the reverse mentoring kicked in. Charmaine had truly inspired Mark and in turn, Mark girded his thirty-five years' of business experience into action in immediate service to CMA. A well-travelled man himself, Mark has made a number of contacts from all walks of life and is in the process of using his network to connect CMA to a source of cheap acupuncture needles. As a casualty insurance underwriter, Mark also latched onto the need for CMA to have the proper liability insurance in place, and he is using core skill-set to solve that problem. Assisting CMA with funding is also on Mark's agenda.

Furthermore, noticing Charmaine's reluctance to publicize CMA in the workplace, Mark took it upon himself to do just that in the final plenary session of our reverse-mentoring scheme. It took place on a Friday, and yes Mark had his Friday shirt on. But when he talked about what he had learned from Charmaine and the work CMA was doing, it was no longer his shirt that was attracting attention. Mark and Charmaine left the scheme with one of its best 'jaw-dropping' moments. Since, then, I know from Charmaine that others in the company have been reaching out to see what they can do to help CMA with its mission.

I am pleased to report that, at the time of writing, Mark and Charmaine's reverse mentoring continues and CMA is planning further projects both in Hong Kong and abroad.

Peter and Kanas

This second case study involves myself as the Generation X mentor being paired with a young lady called Kanas (Generation Y) from our HR department. Both of us were part of the team organizing the scheme, so we decided to put ourselves forward as guinea-pigs by performing our mentorship three months in advance of the timetable's being followed by the rest. That way, when we introduced a new topic to the other mentors, Kanas and I were able to share what we had already discussed, as guidance.

Kanas and I knew each other from our working relationship. The two-way mentoring scheme gave us the opportunity to step beyond this dynamic and learn more about one another's backgrounds.

Probably the first thing one notices about Kanas is that she walks with the aid of crutches, due to a congenital limb disorder. Although I fully expected the subject of Kanas's disability to come up during our discussions, I was reticent about raising it myself. Instead, I decided to hold back and only ask questions about her disability, if she introduced it into our conversations.

This appeared to work. I learned about Kanas's life, her degree in psychology, the work she did outside of the company as part of several NGOs which focused on disability and her deep Christian faith. I learned how Kanas had started to accept speaking engagements at schools, where she would talk about her disability and explain how she had overcome the challenges it posed, to become the successful HR professional she is today. I also learned that one of her goals is to establish an NGO of her own, which could help disabled people make it into the workplace. This was how Kanas answered the question "Why do I do what I do?"

The messages which, I felt, Kanas was trying to get across to me as my mentor were, "Don't judge a book by its cover" and "Just because I'm disabled, don't treat me differently". These were powerful take-aways and I felt the process was working well, until the day I made a rather silly joke.

It happened when Kanas and I were walking together towards the lifts one lunchtime, chatting about our respective workloads, as colleagues do. When we were about ten feet away, the lift doors opened. I jogged forward to hold them. There were people in the lift, whom my action was delaying, so I turned to Kanas, who was making good progress on her crutches, and said, "Hurry up, we haven't got all day!"

It was, as I say, meant as a joke, but there followed several gasps of jaw-dropping horror from my fellow lift passengers, at what they perceived to be a highly insensitive comment. Their reaction immediately ignited my politically correct sensibilities shaming me into a sense embarrassment. I was just about to prostrate myself in apology to Kanas, when I noticed something.

Kanas was laughing. To my utter relief, she was the only person in that lift to find the joke funny.

You see, Kanas got why I had made the joke. She understood that our relationship had now reached a level of familiarity, where I no longer treated her as Kanas my disabled colleague, but as Kanas, my colleague, who just so happens to have a disability. The politically correct way in which I had started out on the process, by avoiding talking about her disability (which in hindsight was stupid) had now been replaced with an entirely different perspective, just from getting to know her. Whilst I knew not to define Kanas by her disability, I had also reached a realization which appreciated that her disability was part of who she was. It influenced her character, her skill-set and her general approach to life. In other words, to define her by her disability was wrong, but to ignore it altogether, equally so.

My joke told Kanas that I finally "got" her, and from that moment on, our reverse-mentoring process took on a different dimension. Discussing her disability was no longer off-limits and by talking about it I learned very much more. Now I had no hesitation about asking questions which previously I had thought were off-limits. For example, I knew Kanas was the lone survivor in our HR department, which had been decimated by an exceptionally high turnover back in 2014. So I asked Kanas, quite bluntly, "Is the reason you stayed because it is difficult for a person with a disability to find another job?"

Kanas confirmed that the Hong Kong business environment was not particularly "disabled-friendly", so opportunities were not easy to come by. But that wasn't why she had stayed. Rather, unlike her colleagues, she had taken a longer-term perspective about her career and realized that with everybody else leaving, she had the opportunity to become the resident force of knowledge on HR issues. All she had to do was be resilient and stick it out through the rocky period. Further, she genuinely liked and felt loyal to the people in the company which had given her the opportunity to work (many companies in Hong Kong would not have done), so it was worth putting up with the disruption for the longer-term pay-off.

In her answer, I saw the different perspective Kanas's disability gave her to the types of challenges we all face in our careers. She also opened my eyes to the very clear business case which exists for adding disabled people to our own workforce, rather than doing so just to be seen to be diverse. I realized that for companies facing problems with high turnover, targeting disabled candidates served as a tangential but obvious solution. In fact, since then Kanas and I have explored the issue further and, at the time of writing, we are working on a plan to attract more disabled candidates to apply for jobs at our company. This typifies the power that reverse mentoring can have.

NOTES

Chapter 4: The origins of reverse mentoring

1 Andy Roberts. 'Homer's Mentor: Duties Fulfilled or Misconstrued' (*History of Education Journal*, November 1999, pp. 81-89.)

Chapter 5: Re-connecting with the child-like mind

2 Adam Zamoyski. *1812 Napoleon's Fatal March on Moscow* - originally published by HarperCollins Publishers 2004, this Kindle edition published by Harper Perennial 2005, first published HarperCollins Publishers, location 8989.

3 Betsy (Elizabeth) Balcombe. *Recollections of the Emperor Napoleon – During the First Three Years Of His Captivity On The Island Of St. Helena.* Originally published in 1845. This edition published on Kindle by Pickle Partners Publishing, 2015, location 284 to 292.

4 *Ibid.*, location 338.

5 *Ibid.*, location 345 to 349.

6 *Ibid.*, location 404 to 413.

7 *Ibid.*, location 413 to 430.

8 *Ibid.*, location 618 to 635.

9 *Ibid.*, location 1632.

10 *Ibid.*, location 1641 to 1666.

11 *Ibid.*, location 1692 to 1710.

12 *Ibid.*, location 1209.

13 *Ibid.*, location 406.

14 *Ibid.*, location 1742.

Chapter 6: The judge and the bookworm

15 *Scott v Sandford*, 60 U.S. 393 (1857)

16 *Plessy v Ferguson*, 163 U.S. 537 (1896)

17 *Brown v Board of Education of Topeka*, 347 U.S. 483 (1954)

18 *Abrams v United States*, 250 U.S. 616 (1919)

19 Abrams, 250 U.S. 616.

20 Thomas Healy. *The Great Dissent: How Oliver Wendell Holmes Changed the History of Free Speech in America.*

Metropolitan Books, Henry Hold and Company New York. 2013.

21 Alexander Adam Seaton. *The Theory of Toleration under the Later Stuarts.* Cambridge University Press, 1911.

22 John Stuart Mill. *On Liberty.* Dover Publications Inc. 2002. First Published 1859.

23 Schenck v United States 249, U.S. 47 (1919)

24 Frohwerk v United States, 249 U.S. 204 (1919)

25 Debs v United States, 249 U.S. 211 (1919)

26 Schenck, 249, U.S. 47 at p. 52.

27 Schenck, 249, U.S. 47 at p. 52.

28 Healy, *op. cit.*, p. 193.

29 *Ibid.*, p. 196.

30 Abrams, 250 U.S. 616 at p. 630.

31 Abrams, 250 U.S. 616 at p. 630.

Chapter 7: The catalyst for change

32 John D'Emilio. *Lost Prophet: The Life and Times of Bayard Rustin.* Free Press, 2003. This book rights this wrong and gives Bayard Rustin his true place in history. It makes for a brilliant and important read.

33 *Ibid.* This moment is related at pp. 326-327.

34 *Ibid.*, p. 339.

35 *Ibid.*, p. 347.

36 *Ibid.*, p. 340.

Chapter 8: The stepping stone to genius

37 Winston Churchill, *My Early Life*, 1930, Eland Press edition 2000, p. 15.

38 *Ibid.*,, pp. 108-111.

39 Max Hastings. *Finest Years, Churchill as Warlord 1940-1945*, HarperPress 2009, pp. 33-35.

40 Daniel Smith. *How to think like Churchill.* Michael O'Mara Books Limited 2015, p. 123.

41 Roy Jenkins. *Churchill*, Pan Books 2002, p. 591.

42 *Ibid.*, p. 611.

43 *Ibid.*, p. 621.

44 Hastings, *op. cit.*, pp. 86-87.

Chapter 9: Achieving true purpose through reverse mentoring

45 Maslow's "Hierarchy of Needs" is brilliantly explained in this piece written by Dr. C. George Boeree, http://webspace.ship.edu/cgboer/maslow.html

46 Patricia Bell-Scott. *The Firebrand and the First Lady*. Alfred A. Knopf 2016, Kindle Edition. This brilliant and superbly researched book relates the story of the unlikely friendship between Pauli Murray and Eleanor Roosevelt.

47 *Ibid.,* location 4154.

48 *Ibid.,* location 5539.

49 *Ibid.,* location 5764 to 5775.

50 *Ibid.,* location 4776.

51 *Ibid.,* location 5627.

Chapter 10: The art of constant study

52 C.G. Jung. *Memories, Dreams, Reflections, recorded and edited by Aniela Jaffe*, New York: Vintage Books, 1989.

53 Walter Isaacson. *Benjamin Franklin, An American Life*, Simon & Shuster Paperbacks, p. 252.

54 *Ibid.*, p. 92.

55 *Ibid.*, pp. 176-177.

56 For information on 'The Learning Pyramid', see the link below
http://thepeakperformancecenter.com/educational-learning/learning/principles-of-learning/learning-pyramid/

57 Robert Greene. *Mastery*. Viking 2012, pp. 119-121.

58 Ryan Holiday. *Ego is the Enemy*. Portfolio Penguin 2016, location 578 to 618.

Chapter 11: The summer of 1997

59 Andrew Duguid. *On The Brink: How a crisis transformed Lloyd's of London*. Palgrave Macmillan 2014, p. 3.

60 Adam Raphael. *Ultimate Risk*, Corgi 1995, pp. 219-220.

61 The story of the development and implementation of this business plan is brilliantly related in Andrew Duiguid's book *On The Brink: How a crisis transformed Lloyd's of London* – see note 59 above.

Chapter 12: The benefits of reverse mentoring

62 Russell Miller. *Uncle Bill: The Authorised Biography of Field Marshall Viscount Slim*, Phoenix 2014, p. 339.

63 *Ibid.*, pp. 225 - 226.

64 K. Anders Ericsson and Robert Pool. *Peak. Secrets from the New Science of Expertise*, An Eamon Dolan Book, Kindle Edition, 2016 location 1902 to 1933.

Additional note

Le Mémorial de Saint-Hélène by Count Emmanuel de Las Casas is the four-volume memoir of Napoleon's life referenced in Chapter 5. Las Casas first published *Le Mémorial* in 1823 and went on to republish it several times during his life-time. A recent English version of *Le Mémorial* was published by Pickle Partners Publishing in 2013, entitled *Memoirs of the Life, Exile, And Conversations of the Emperor Napoleon* – Vol I. to IV", and can be found as a kindle edition.

FIND OUT MORE ABOUT PROVERSE AUTHORS, BOOKS, EVENTS AND LITERARY PRIZES

Visit our website: http://www.proversepublishing.com

Visit our distributor's website: <www.chineseupress.com>

Follow us on Twitter
Follow news and conversation: twitter.com/Proversebooks>
OR
Copy and paste the following to your browser window and follow the instructions: https://twitter.com/#!/ProverseBooks

"Like" us on www.facebook.com/ProversePress

Request our free E-Newsletter
Send your request to info@proversepublishing.com.

Availability
Most titles are available in Hong Kong and world-wide from our Hong Kong based Distributor, The Chinese University of Hong Kong Press, The Chinese University of Hong Kong, Shatin, NT, Hong Kong SAR, China. Email: cup-bus@cuhk.edu.hk Website: <www.chineseupress.com>.

All titles are available from Proverse Hong Kong, http://www.proversepublishing.com and the Proverse Hong Kong UK-based Distributor.

Stock-holding retailers
Hong Kong (Growhouse, Bookazine) Singapore (Select Books), Canada (Elizabeth Campbell Books), Andorra (Llibreria La Puça, La Llibreria). **Orders from bookshops** in the UK and elsewhere.

Ebooks
Many of our titles are available also as Ebooks.